Joe Robinson

A Cowboy's Life

Recorded and Transcribed by Noel Logan

Edited by Aaron Logan

This is a work of non-fiction/photography. Names, characters, places, and incidents either are the product of the author's experiences, the course of events, or are used fictitiously. Any resemblance to actual persons, living or dead, events, or locales is entirely coincidental.

Copyright © 2024 by Iconic Book Publishers

All rights reserved. No part of this book may be reproduced or used in any manner without the written permission of the copyright owner except for the use of brief quotations in a book review.

First edition, August 2024
Book Published® by Mr. Adam Benson

PRINTED IN THE IN THE UNITED STATES OF AMERICA

CONTENTS

* **PREFACE** 9

* **FIRST IMPRESSIONS** 11

* **EARLY LIFE IN TEXAS** 30

* **A YOUNG COWBOY IN TEXAS** 43

* **LEAVING TEXAS** 47

* **ARIZONA** 50

* **RED CANYON RANCH** 105

* **IN DUE TIME** 108

ABOUT THE AUTHOR

Aaron Logan is a third-generation Arizonan who was born in Flagstaff and was raised in the Sedona and Verde Valley. he grew up mostly at Red Canyon Ranch with his dad, who was the caretaker at the time.

Aaron received a BA in creative writing from the University of Arizona in Tucson. Once deciding that the city life was not for him, he went to work in Marble Canyon where he met his wife. He has worked in archaeology, construction and as a mechanic for Grand Canyon River Outfitters.

He currently lives with his wife on the Navajo Reservation and his family cares for the livestock and horses devotedly. In substitution, he also teaches and cuts firewood for his cattle.

DEDICATIONS

This book is dedicated to my dad, who had the vision and foresight to record Joe's story on a tape recorder over forty years ago. In doing so, he captured an important and fleeting time in Arizona history. Through wanderings and adventures and assorted adventures with my dad, a love of horses and wilderness was instilled in me at a young age.

I hope, in some way, this book expresses my gratitude for all he has done and all he has given me.

NOTE TO MY READER

My interest in writing this book was the preservation of firsthand accounts of Arizona's cowboy history.

Place names and geographical locations play an important role in interpreting this history, as it mostly takes place on public lands.

And because Joe had an impeccable memory for place names, his personal account became an important part of a larger collection of Arizona historical resources.

First Impressions by Aaron Logan

Written from notes and recorded conversations.

between my dad and Joe

PREFACE

This book is the story of Joe Robinson, an Arizona traditional working cowboy.

Joe was a cowboy in the traditional sense, being born in Texas in 1911 and going to work as a cowboy at an early age. He experienced trail drives across open range, following chuck wagons in West Texas and eventually made his way to Arizona. Throughout time, he witnessed dramatic changes in the cattle industry and learned to adapt to those changes.

Joe had been a cowboy his entire life and never worked full-time in any other profession. Never becoming disillusioned or dissatisfied with his life as a cowboy, he represents the typical "old-timer" in his subculture.

The golden age of the cowboy disappeared with the coming of the twentieth century, but the cowboy subculture remained alive and strong in the West American. The cowboy subculture was not a socially imposed fringe culture of backward or economically inferior people. Instead, it is a self-imposed subculture of independent, self-sufficient, and for the most part, a very satisfied people. Although there are a few working cowboys around today, their influence on the history of Arizona is still very strong. Family names like Babbitt, Sullivan, and Lockett played important roles in the growth and development of Northern Arizona.

The life of the cowboy has greatly changed since it first began in the nineteenth century. The loss of free use of land is perhaps the greatest change. In the early days, ranges were unfenced and open. Today, private ranches utilize federally controlled land through the use of grazing permits. Despite all these changes, the main focus of a cowboy's attention is still the cow.

Joe Robinson's life perfectly represents that of the traditional cowboy, and his life story contains several common themes. Horses, the love of all cowboys. Cattle, the focus of their work. Food and shelter are all a cowboy expects from life, and finally, nature. Nature and the American wilderness played a large role in the daily existence of a cowboy. This way of life, as seen from a modern perspective, is very appealing and is the reason the Myth of the West and the cowboy subculture lives on.

FIRST IMPRESSIONS

I first met Joe Robinson in the spring of 1978.

I had saddled my big mare, Blackie, for a long ride towards Black Tank in the beautiful red rock country west of Sedona. We lived at the end of the pavement on Dry Creek Road, where it turned to dirt. From there, it was all National Forest for miles, including Sycamore Canyon Wilderness area and Secret Mountain Wilderness. I had ridden around eight miles or so, on several occasions to the gate and cattle guard of Red Canyon Ranch. This day, I spotted an old cowboy working with a pick and shovel, repairing the roadbed at the cattle guard. Parked nearby was an old beat-up GMC, three-quarter-ton pickup. I rode up to say, "howdy." The old cowboy looked up my horse and then down and said, "I sure like the looks of your pony." I got off Blackie and introduced ourselves.

Joe was a big, powerful man and looked every bit the old-time cowboy. He wore a well-used black Stetson hat, a light-colored long sleeve, a pearl-snap shirt, Levi's, and high-heeled, low-topped boots that were not too pointy. At the time, he was sixty-seven years old. His hair was thin and white, and because of the light complexion of his skin, his face and hands were covered with dark sunspots. Over six feet tall, he must have weighed 250 pounds. His hands were large and rough from a lifetime of handling livestock.

We sat in the shade of a tree and began to talk with the familiarity of old friends. Joe's favorite subjects were horses and cows in general, horse and cow anatomy, and psychology in particular. He also liked to note the weather and make observations about the condition of the *"range"* and other natural phenomena.

Joe took his pouch of Bull Durham rolling tobacco from his breast pocket and built himself a cigarette as we sat and talked. I quickly learned that he also used Copenhagen snuff and Days o' Work plug tobacco. Sometimes, at the same time, I could see the tell-tale brown tobacco juice leaking from the corner of his mouth as he lit his hand-rolled cigarette. He called this drool "embers," referring to its color. He used smoking as a good excuse to take a break, and he didn't like to smoke alone. I couldn't roll a decent roll-your-own. So, on several occasions, throughout our friendship, he would roll one for me. His technique was to pack the paper with loose-leaf tobacco and roll it between his fingers like a pencil. After he licked the glue on the side of the paper, he put the whole thing in his mouth and pulled it out slowly. When he handed it to me, it would be dripping wet with spit and Copenhagen juice. I usually had to let it dry a minute or so before it could be lit.

At that time, I was thirty-one years old, but Joe started calling me "Bud" right off. It was a term of endearment, and he reserved it for young people he liked. Little did I know that this was the start of a long friendship that would be one of the most deeply rewarding I would ever have. Although he continued to call me *Bud* for the rest of the time I knew him. The best compliment I ever got from him was years later when he introduced me to some of his old cowboy friends as "Noel, a good hand."

During that first visit, I learned that he and his wife, Dolly, had recently sold Red Canyon Ranch and were moving to Sedona. To both of our surprise, we learned he had just bought the house and property next door to me and my family. Joe and Dolly had lived at Red Canyon for the last thirty years and had recently sold it to the Coconino National Forest. Joe needed to live near town because of Dolly's poor health, and the NFS wanted the ranch because it contains a big prehistoric site: large petroglyph panels and a two-story Sinagua cliff dwelling.

I helped them move into the house on Dry Creek by loading all their furniture into his old four-horse trailer and hauling it to the new place on Dry Creek Road. Later, we went back for his horses. I also helped build his barn and horse corrals. Joe and I became close friends, and he soon invited me to work with him at the DK Ranch in the Verde Valley. Joe had worked off and on for the DK since 1943; at the time, it was his full-time job. This was a wonderful opportunity because I studied Western art and bronze casting and hoped to gather material and photographs for my art. But instead of being the observer I had anticipated; I quickly became a participant in the Arizona cowboy subculture.

Over the years, Joe taught me a great deal about horses, cattle, and ranch work. He always demonstrated great patience and willingness to teach me some fine points or methods involved with tending cattle. His knowledge of horses and cattle were limitless, and he shared it freely with me. However, what I learned most over the years was that contrary to public perception, cowboy culture is not a socially imposed culture of uneducated, economically depressed people. Instead, it is a self-imposed subculture of very independent and hard-working people who derive their satisfaction in life from their love of horses, cattle, the outdoors, and family. Their quality of life is determined by the health and well-being of these four important aspects. The accumulation of wealth has never been a high priority for the working cowboy.

It was early spring of 1980, when I had my first day of "cowboyin'" with Joe. It was still dark, and I was in the kitchen, finishing my coffee, when I heard his old four-horse trailer banging down the dirt lane. We loaded my mare, Blackie, into the trailer with his two horses; one was a big gray mare he called "Whitey," and the other was a chestnut mare called "Star" because there of the white star or snip on her forehead. They were both about sixteen and seventeen years old.

Joe was trying to get his Australian shepherd cow-dog, "Misty," back in the horse trailer. She had come out to say hello to my little blue healer named, "Lupita."

"Come on, Misty, come on, bad girl! Get up in that trailer with them horses!" His dog jumped in, and mine quickly followed.

I had a small tape recorder with me in the interest of recording our conversations, and with his permission, I turned it on as I climbed into the cab of his truck. It smelled like leather, Copenhagen tobacco, and cigarette smoke. I think Joe might have been a little reluctant to have a greenhorn along, but he was cheerful and seemed glad to have the company. We were headed for the Windmill Ranch, about fifteen miles away, the winter headquarters for the DK Ranch. We drove quietly for a few minutes until we crossed over Dry Creek bridge, where Joe noted it was running.

"Old Dry Creek sure is running. Had lots of snow up on the mountain this winter." About that time, I spotted a bald eagle lit on top of a dead juniper tree.

"Hey, look, Joe. There's a big eagle sitting in that tree right there."

"Oh, yeah. I'd seen one around here ever so often. One of them is brown eagles. "No, look. This one is a bald eagle."

"Oh, a bald eagle. I'll be damned. You know, at one time, there used to be a pair of bald eagles living next to that pond in Frye Park."

There was a ten-or-fifteen-minute pause in the conversation."Kind of warm for early April," I said.

"Yeah, but we know damn well spring isn't here yet. I've seen it be this way in March and then turn off and be so damned cold and snowy and April and May. Haven't you?"

"Oh, hell yeah."

"I sure love it, though," he said.

"It doesn't really get warm up on the mountain until way into June sometimes," I said.

"Yeah, unless you're working on them damn fences out in the jack-pine forest."

Joe paused a few minutes.

We were slowing down for our turn-off from the highway. Joe pointed to the North and said, "Bud, I hear up there at the windmill and tank; they got a hippy nest up there. Old George (George Fisher, the DK manager) says them bastards, built themselves a house of some kind up there. I guess there are two or three families up there with a bunch of kids running around."

We drove down the dirt road a mile or so when Joe offered me some advice for the day. "Well, Bud, I guess you never worked on a ranch before, so let me give you some ranchin' advice before we get there. First, don't pay a damn bit of attention to what the manager tells you. He ain't my boss, and he damn sure ain't your boss. Now, I've seen you around horses, and you move quiet and easy. That's the way you need to be around the cattle, too.

Always work the cattle at a walk or you'll spread them all over the place. Stay behind the cows 'cause you'll have to watch 'em at all times. If you're not, you won't be able to out-guess which way they run. Watch me all the time, and I'll tell you what you need tobe doin.' Stay back of me unless I ask you to go ahead.

Don't let your dog chase or bark at the cows or horses. If she does, you'll have to take her back to the truck and lock her up in the horse trailer. If she watches my dog Misty, she'll learn a lot. If we got someone else ridin' with us, don't ride too close to 'em or cut 'em off. It just ain't polite.

And when we come to a gate, the first one there can get down and open it. If you go through the gate first, stay close by. If you ride off, my horse might try to follow you and leave me a foot. That might really piss me off. So, do not do that.

If we need to make a cut in the herd, you stay back and hold 'em, and I'll do the cuttin.' Also, don't rope unless I ask you to. I'll give you a chance, but I'll handle most of the ropin.'

Oh, yeah, one last thing: watch out for the stallions on the allotments. There's a couple of 'em that are mean as hell. If they come around, take down your rope and slap 'em on the nose if they get too close...Is that all okay with you?"

Joe appeared to be wondering if he'd missed anything but remained quiet.

"I think I got it," I said. It was a lot of information, but mostly just common sense.

That day, we worked with just the two of us. It was a pleasure to ride with Joe and watch him work. We had to move about forty cows and their bawling calves four miles to the south end of the allotment, where they would be closer to better feed and water. Those wily cows would break away from the head and take off running. It seemed like Joe knew which direction they were thinking of going and headed them off at a gallop or even a dead run before turning them back into the herd. He sat tall in the saddle and made it look effortless. Of course, his horse was also well-versed in out-guessing cows and was just as impressive. It was all Blackie, and I could do to keep up at first. Every time I just finished hazing one back into the herd, another would pop out the other side.

Joe's dog, Misty, was barking and nipping at the heels of the cows to keep them going in the right direction. Lupita, my blue healer, was catching on fast. After a while, the cattle settled down, and it was mostly a matter of keeping the stragglers moving and to keep them from stopping to graze.

Later that day, Joe's curiosity got the best of him, so we took a break from our ranch tasks to ride to the windmill where the "hippy nest" was. We left the cows milling around grazing at whatever was found near a water tank there. Then we rode to the windmill and found a large camp with a couple of families living in an old school bus surrounded by tents. They said they were looking for work in Cottonwood and were planning to move as soon as they could find a place. Despite Joe's rough talk earlier, he was nice as could be to all of them. He got down off his horse, shook hands with everyone, and introduced himself and me. The next thing I knew, he was giving the kids rides on his mare and sharing hand-rolled smokes with the men. He told them they could stay as long as they wanted as long as they didn't chase cows away from the water and to watch out for George, the manager.

As we rode away, Joe clucked his tongue and expressed heartfelt concern for "them poor families."

I rode with Joe several days a week for almost nine years, and I became his right-hand man. I had finished my master's in anthropology, and as a struggling Western artist, I had plenty of free time to work with Joe.

One chilly morning, Joe and I were driving twenty or so cows and calves ahead of us. We were moving them to a new pasture where better grass could be had. We found this bunch balled up together in the fence corner of the northwest end of the allotment. They had been without water for a couple of days and were just too stupid to move out of that corner. It was a self-imposed trap they were in. We hazed them out and turned them south to the allotment along lower Oak Creek. It was a cold, long ride, but Joe was in a talkative mood and in good spirits.

"Hey, Bud, you know any old-time cowboy songs?"

I told him I knew a few verses of the "Strawberry Roan." It had been a favorite of my dad's, who knew all the verses by heart.

"Well, hell! Sing it for me."

I gave it a try, even though I couldn't carry a tune for trying:

Well, I'm standin' 'round town just wastin' my time.

Out of a job, I ain't got a dime.

When this 'ol boy steps up an' says,

'I suppose that you're a bronc twister by the rig of your clothes'....

The ballad goes on, and I could only remember some of the verses. I got to the part where the cowboy gets ready to mount the bronc...

Then I step aboard him and pulls off the blinds,

and I take a deep seat just to feel him unwind....

There is where my memory failed entirely, and I couldn't recall the rest of that verse or any other.

"Shit, that's where it just started to get good," Joe said.

We both laughed and spent some time trying to remember the other verses as we rode along. The cows were moving along well, but every now and then, a "grass-bellied scalawag" would break out and get a hold of a green yucca stalk. The cattle loved green yucca stalks, and if they spotted one in the distance, they would break loose and charge it at a dead run. Then they would cram the top of the blossom and the stalk as far down their throats before they bit it off. Until they had that stalk in their belly, you could not get them to move. Because I was still considered the greenhorn, it was my job to chase after the stragglers and haze them back into the herd. Those damn yuccas kept me running back and forth behind the herd most of the day. When things settled down a bit, I told Joe it was his turn to sing a song.

He laughed and asked, "Have you ever heard the song 'Little Joe Wrangler?'"

"No," I said.

He didn't sing it, instead it was more like reciting poetry. He also only knew a few verses. However, the lyrics to Little Wrangler Joe are readily available as they were popularized along with "Strawberry Roan" by country singer Marty Robins. Here is part of the first and last ballad:

It was little Joe the wrangler, he'll wrangle never more,

His days with the horses, they are done.

Was a year ago last summer he rode up to the herd,

just a little Texas stray and all alone...

...Next mornin' just at sun-up we found where Rocket felldown in a wash-

out forty feet below.

Beneath his horse smashed to a pulp, his spurs had rung the knell. For

our little lost herder, wrangler Joe.

Joe could only remember a few verses, and we tried to recall more as we rode along. I could see why Little Joe the Wrangler had stuck with Joe, being from Texas himself and once a "button."

*****

It was the spring of 1987, the runoff was coming from the rim country, and all the usually dry creeks were flowing pretty good. We were heading out to Black Tank near Sycamore Pass. Sycamore Canyon being the center of an enormous wilderness area. There were some Brahma bulls that had broken through the barbed wire fence and out of the grazing allotment. Joe and I had to find where they broke out, ride through, find them, and get them back into the allotment. We quickly found the break in the fence and easily tracked them to the pass that looked down into Sycamore Canyon, a sandstone wilderness of canyons.

"Damn, we ought to be up at Taylor Cabin. I'll bet the water's really running in Sycamore Creek right now," Joe said.

"Why don't we do that someday, Joe?"

"Well, we'd better do it this spring. Goddamn, I'm going to get too old."

"You pick the time, and I'd sure go with you."

"You will?" Joe pauses for a moment, "May's probably a better time 'cause it's still gettin' awful cold in that damn cabin at night, and I ain't riding in there just to turn around the same day. When we get there, I want to stay there for a day or two. In fact, I'd like to go in there for about a week or two. Ride plum up to Winter Cabin and then go around under the hill to Dorsey Springs and then Geronimo Springs, and Kelsey Springs and out on top that way."

We rode along for a while and Joe appeared to be thinking hard about something. "You know, Bud. That's where I want to go when I die someday."

"Where's that, Joe?"

"Oh, just somewhere up Sycamore. You know, I have this cancer. (Joe had recently been diagnosed with prostate cancer.) Would you ride up there with me when the time comes, Bud? I sure don't want to die in one of them damn hospitals."

"Why sure, Joe! You know I will, but you ain't going to die for a long time."

We rode and tracked those bulls up the side of Casner Mountain, where we found them in thick brush and prickly pear—chasing those two bulls back through proved to be a chore because it was *real* rough country.

Not only was it steep and rocky, but the scrub oak and prickly pear were so thick that our horses were having a hard time. Where the bulls could go crashing through, we had to ride around.

Every time, we had them headed for the busted fence. They would break back out the opposite way, up the hillside through the brush. These old bulls were smart and half-wild. It took some "tall" riding, and I watched Joe work; you would never guess he was a man in his seventies. With the help of our dogs, we finally hazed those brutes through the fence and made the necessary repairs.

Working cattle in May, in the Verde Valley of Central Arizona can be pretty damn hot. It was spring round-up, and Joe and I were staying busy, gathering cattle on the far north end of the allotment. We were moving them to the holding pens at Gyber Tank just outside of Cottonwood. There, they would be kept in the pens until we could get them loaded into livestock trailers and hauled to the summer pastures of the mountain. What Joe and other old-timers in the Verde Valley referred to as the "mountain" was the high country to the north. This country is on the far western edge of the Mogollon Rim. It includes extensive ponderosa pine forests and deep grassy meadows. It's perfect for cattle in the summertime, and it's where the DK Ranch had its summer headquarters at

Rodger's Dry Lake, just southwest of Flagstaff.

We had been riding all morning, and the sun had been really cooking us. We were close to a windmill and a large water storage tank.

"Hey, you want to go swimming?" Joe asked.

The storage tank was made of steel, above ground, and about six feet high. It was full of cool, clear water. The cattle drank from concrete troughs below.

"Hell yeah! But how are we going to get in there? We don't have a ladder or anything." Joe had already stepped off his mare and was pulling his boots and chaps off.

"Well, get your britches off. We'll get in there by standin' on our horses," Joe said.

We both proceeded to strip down to our underwear, and then I tied my mare to the windmill derrick. We tied Joe's mare to a pipe fitting that stuck out from the tank. She was gentle, and we knew she would stand still for us if we stood on her back. I pushed the mare as close to the tank as I could, and then Joe climbed up on her. From there, it was easy for him to pull himself over the top of the tank and into the water. I heard a loud splash and a "Yahoo!" from the other side. Joe was swimming around and splashing by the time I got into the water. The water was cold at first, then just very refreshing. I had no idea that Joe could swim. He managed a steady dogie paddle. He laughed and played and kept trying to sneak up behind and dunk me.

When we were tired of paddling around, we draped our arms over the tank's edge and hung them by our armpits. The windmill was on high ground, and we had a great view of Cottonwood to the southwest. The hot sunshine warmed out our heads and shoulders. We must have been a sight. Two white balding heads peaking over the top of that old water tank.

It began to occur to me that it might be a chore to get this 250-pound, 76-year-old man out of this water tank. When I brought it up, he already had the answer.

"Well, you know, Bud, I could pull myself over the top if I had something to stand on."

I knew what he meant, and I took a deep breath, plunged under water, and squatted down in front of Joe. He climbed on my shoulders, and for what seemed like a long time, I wondered just how long I would be able to stay under. Finally, I felt him lift himself off my back. I came up for air and found Joe hanging by one leg halfway over the edge of the tank.

"Bud, you're going to have to pull me over."

I knew I couldn't push him over because his horse would probably shy out of the way.

The six-foot fall would hurt Joe badly, so I pulled myself up and over the tank edge and lowered myself to the ground. I coaxed his horse against the tank and climbed on top of the saddle. I was able to pull Joe over the edge and guide his legs to the seat of the saddle. Now, we both stood dripping wet in our underwear on the back of his horse as we steadied ourselves by holding on to the rim of the tank. If his horse had decided to do something as much as move, we both would have been hurt. But Joe always kept a sound, calm horse. I climbed back to the edge of the tank and steadied Joe as he eased back into the saddle. I jumped off the tank, Joe climbed off his horse, and we dressed. We sat in the shade and laughed at ourselves.

"Joe, have you ever had any regrets about being a full-time cowboy your whole life?"

"Hell, no! Not once, ever!" Joe proclaimed.

JOE AT DK RANCH 1983

In 1987, Joe Robinson was diagnosed with cancer. While he received treatment for prostate and bone marrow cancer, we spent less time on horseback. It was during this time, usually at his kitchen table, over coffee and a pack of hand-rolled cigarettes, that I recorded Joe telling his life story. What follows are his own words:

EARLY LIFE IN TEXAS

I was born Joseph Warren Robinson, on the thirteenth of September, 1911. I was born way out on the prairie in a little old cabin, a long way from any town. I was told that my momma did it all alone as my daddy was out taking care of livestock. The nearest town was Rotan, which must have been thirty miles. My daddy was called J.A., and my momma's name was Kate. I had two sisters, both older than me, and a younger brother named Stanley. Stanley just died last Christmas (1984). He was four years younger, and I'm the last one of the outfits left.

My momma and daddy were real nice to us kids. My daddy was kind of a dark, short guy–a small man. He raised horses and cattle, too. 'Course me and my "Bud" (brother) broke every damn colt that was born. When we got big enough, we got to runnin' wild burros. We broke all of them burros and just gave 'em away. We sure had our share of kicks and broken bones.

My momma was a tall, big lady. She was light-skinned and always nice to us all. There were four of us kids and both our parents were real nice. I never heard my momma and daddy have an argument. I'm not saying they didn't, just not in front of me. Neither one was ever cross and both were very kind natured.

My daddy was an old-time cowpuncher ahead of me. He was born in California about 1875, I think. His folks went out there from Alabama in an ox-drawn wagon. My grandpa was a freighter in the early days. He went over to California during the gold rush, and when the money got short, I guess about 1890 or so, he pulled out and moved back to Texas. He had ox and mule teams, and my daddy helped him out for a while 'till he got big enough to go punchin' cows. Daddy said when he was just a kid helping his daddy freight, most of what they were haulin' was salt and barbed wire. They'd connect three or four wagons together and make two teams. One team was driven by oxen, and the other team driven by mules. When they got in mud, the oxen would out-walk the mules. When they crossed sand, the mules would out-walk the oxen.

I don't know how old my daddy was at the time, but my grandpa was murdered. He went to feed the stock one morning, and somebody shot him in the back with a shotgun. I never did know why. The old guy who did it, his name was Johnson. I never did know why he did it. I guess there was some bad blood between them–probably money.

My daddy taught me a few good things, like breaking horses, but I left home so early he didn't have a chance to teach me much else. My Uncle Jim taught me more than anybody. Everything else I just picked up on my own.

My momma and her parents were all born in Texas. I remember my momma tried to go to church when she could. But we lived so far out she couldn't go that often. My momma and sisters were pretty religious and read the Bible every night. My daddy would never go to church, and when I was just a button, I would only go when my momma made me. Both my momma and daddy could read and write, and my momma wrote letters to me all her life. Sure, I'd write her back as often as I could. They were real kind and nice and did everything they could for us kids.

My folks owned a small ranch outside of Rotan. My grandpa had owned it and when he and grandma died, the place went to all the kids. My daddy inherited only a part of it, so it just sat there all his life. After my daddy died, the family settled up on it. They sent me my part of the money, but I wouldn't take it. I didn't need it and would have just blown it anyway. I gave my part to my momma.

Before all that, my folks owned a small ranch of their own near Rotan. My daddy sold that to buy a cow outfit in New Mexico. That's when we started to move around a lot. We went to myuncle's house in New Mexico, where he owned a pretty big cow outfit. We'd only been in New Mexico for about a year when Momma said she wanted to go back home to Texas.

So, we went back to Rotan and lived with another one of my uncles for three or four years. That's when I went to school. Went to school way out. Walked or sometimes rode fir miles each way. It was just a little one room schoolhouse with twenty or thirty students in it - mostly Mexican kids. I can't remember any of my teacher's names.

It was around that time; my daddy bought another place about fifteen miles or so from town. It was more of a farm because it had pasture-land on it, too. I quit school about that time to help my daddy in the place, which was fine with me because I was a lot more interested in horses and cows than in reading or writing. But my daddy went broke, and we picked up and moved again, this time to a place where we more or less stayed. It was here I started to hang out with some friends who I had met in school. They used to come and see me and stay all night, and I'd go see them and stay all night with them. I had horses, and they had horses, and we got out and rode a lot.

During that time, me and a couple of other boys took off on what we called a wild cow hunt. In those days, we could go out and find unbranded cattle that had been missed by other roundups. We could make a little money this way by returning them to the ranch owners. Most of the time, my parents didn't know where I was. That's when my daddy died when I was on a wild cow hunt. He died, I believe, of a stroke or a heart attack. I think I was around ten or eleven years old then. Although, we pretty much had family scattered all across Texas, we didn't get together very often 'cause we lived so far out. An old wagon was the only way we had to travel with the family. The uncle we lived with when we came back from New Mexico was an old bachelor who had never married. He wasn't really a cowboy, I guess he was more or less a horse trader and farmer.

We were living with him when my daddy took us kids fishing on the Double Mountain Fork of the Brazos River. We put a wagon sheet on the wagon, and the whole family went. We packed the bottom of the wagon with grub, bedrolls, feather beds, tarps, quilts and dutch ovens. Me and my brother rode our ponies, and the rest of the outfit piled into the wagon. We had flour, beans, coffee, sugar, and bacon stuffed into a barrel. Momma would make us hot dutch oven biscuits and bacon in the morning. We would slather one of her homemade jams on those warm biscuits and boy, they were good! We also had some fresh beef.

I liked catching those ugly catfish but would not eat 'em. We had no real fishing gear except for some big hooks we tied on to heavy cord. We used worms and bacon fat for bait and tossed 'em in and let 'em sink to the bottom. I remember that was the first time Momma let me try coffee, 'course with a lot of sugar in it. We camped out about six or seven days and had a lotof fun. I was probably about six or seven by then and can remember we went quite a way out.

I first started cowboyin' when I was in the fifth grade. About that time, we had a school bus to ride into Rotan. When I got into town, I always had to go to one of my cousin's houses to wait for school to start. She was a schoolmarm and made me feel uncomfortable. It seemed like I was never clean enough or mannerly enough to be in her house. Then, when I got home, my daddy had heard from the schoolmarm about how bad I was, and I'd get a good switchtin'. I was told I'd better calm down. Hell, I didn't want to calm down, so I just got up and quit school. I saddled up my pony and went to my Uncle Jim's on my momma's side about fifteen miles away.

He was runnin' a ranch, and I was just a little kid when I showed up. My uncle always treated me good and helped me out whenever he could.

I remember one time for my birthday, I must have been eleven or twelve, he gave me a sixty-foot Mexican made lariat. I was sure proud of that thing. Well, I commenced to ropin' everything–dogs, chickens, burros and even people if they got within range. I was feeling pretty ornery one day and roped the old outhouse with my cousin in it. I dallied the rope and put the spurs to my old pony and pulled that shitter right over. I got a lickin' that night and had to eat my meals on the back porch for a couple of days. I stayed around with my uncle that year– 'course I didn't draw no wages. But that winter he put me on the payroll to feed a bunch of bulls and cut firewood with an ax. That next spring, an old boy runnin' another ranch nearby had put up a lot of hay. He came by and asked my uncle if I could cut hay for him that summer. I stayed on most of the summer 'till I got tired of that, then went back to work for my uncle. I worked there for a year or two.

One winter, the outfit had balled up a big bunch of cows in a great big pasture down on the Brazos River. I fed them cake seed all winter and, in the spring, they were sold. That's when I started on my first trail drive.

We had to take this herd way up west of that country and plum up on the plains to put them on a certain railroad. I must have been thirteen at the time and we had somewhere between three and four hundred head of cattle. These cows were calving every day on the trail. Me, being a kid, it was my job to pack those little old calves. Every day, I'd pack a damn calf on the front of my saddle from one bedding ground to the next. We'd only do about five miles a day. That's about when we got into a hell of a snowstorm. The horses all got away except one horse apiece because we always kept those tied up at night. We took off trackin' them damn horses in that awful snowstorm. We caught up with some and caught a few, maybe two or three a piece. By the end of the night after riding and looking for our horses, we had all the wet and cold we could take. We figured the rest of them were heading back to the main ranch anyway, so we said to hell with it and let 'em go. We kept heading for the railroad.

We were in a big pasture up there and had forty or fifty bulls. Those bulls had been riding them poor cows and causing a lot of trouble–springtime, you know. So, they cut all those bulls out in one bunch and sent me to the railroad with 'em by myself. I had nothing but trouble and could not keep those old bulls bunched up. They kept drifting off one or two at a time; then another bunch would take off into a trot or run. I think mostly they were tired and wanted to be left alone so they could graze. I finally got this bunch coursed out for the railroad. But it sure was a job for a kid.

  We slept outside with our bedroll and tarp but couldn't keep dry no matter how hard we tried. When it's cold in that country, it's really cold. The whole drive took about a month. I got all the dirty jobs the kids always did. I rode drag–in the back of the herd–all the time. I also stood guard at night, just like the other men. Everybody got from two to four hours of guard every night to watch the horses we kept hobbled out. We each had our winter horses, about three each to start with, but we had already lost some in the snowstorm. Every night, we tied up a horse a piece. There weren't many fences to worry about and generally, there was plenty of water. After that drive, I went back to my Uncle Jim's place and worked for him for about a year. That spring, I was camped out with the wagon. There, they dehorned all those calves and cauterized 'em with a horn-searing iron to stop the bleeding. Well, that's how I burnt my leg when I was just a kid. I dropped one of them red-hot irons on my leg. The burn infected from my dirty old Levi's rubbin' on it, and I got blood poisoning out there with the wagon. So, they took me to a doctor in Rotan. I don't remember much; I guess I almost died. I stayed with my momma for two or three months 'till I could move around again. But after a while, I went back to my uncle's place.

I was still on the mend but could ride some when my Uncle Jim came to me and said, "I've got to leave for now for a while. It's going to be up to you."

My uncle did all the cookin,' so he showed me how to make biscuits, how to make coffee, how to fry potatoes and bacon and other stuff like that. He was gone about forty days. I never figure out where he went. I think he was probably chasing women but will never know for sure.

I might have been about fourteen years old, and here I was all alone out on this big ranch. There were an awful lot of screwworms in the cattle that year. So, all I did all day, every day, was doctor screwworms. I doctored 'em where I'd found 'em. When I saw a cow with worms, I'd rope her, tie her down, and doctor her with a regular worm medicine called Peerless.

Most of the time doctorin' screw worms wasn't so bad. But every once in a while, I'd have taken care of screwworms in a baby calf. That's when things can get pretty scary. Some of those old cows were half wild and with a little Brahman in 'em–maybe even a little Longhorn. Cows can be awful protective of their calves. I had roped a calf and had it tied down on the ground when the old momma threw a fit. At first, I thought she was just going to do a lot of ballerina' and dancin' around just to put a bluff on me. She made a couple of fake charges at me, but I wasn't too worried. But on the third or fourth charge, she went right over me. I went head over heels but wasn't hurt too badly. I could see she was fixin' to charge me again, and I was afraid she might be able to snag me with one of those damn sharp horns. I took off a runnin,' and just as I got to my horse, she hit me again. This time, the horn just caught my leg as I was swinging up onto the saddle. By then, I was pretty scared, but being on horseback, I was able to avoid any more charges. But now I had the calf tied to the ground needin' doctorin.' It took a while to drive the momma far enough away so I could do my doctorin.' When I was done, I cleaned up my leg. She had horned my right leg, back of the thigh–it hurt like hell! I cleaned it as best as I could and tied it up with an old piece of shirt. It was sure sore and tender for a while, but it never got infected.

During this time by myself, I got hurt again. This time, my horse stepped in a dog hole (prairie dog) and tumbled. I fell clear but busted up my shoulder and broke my collarbone. This was winter, long about January or February, and it was windy and cold as hell! I couldn't lift my arm, and it hurt to do anything. I managed to get me and my horse back to the cabin, but that was about all I could do. Getting the saddle off the horse about killed me. After that, there wasn't much to do but try and stay warm. I had no way to get a hold of anyone for help. 'Course, I don't know what anybody could have done for me. Anyway, after a couple of weeks, I started to feel better. I just had to go easy on my left arm. Soon, I was back to doctorin' cows.

One night, there by myself, I was taking a bath in a washtub in the middle of the cabin. It must have been below zero outside, and the wind was howlin.' There was a door on the north side of the house and a door on the south side. Well, I was sittin' there enjoying the warm water I had heated on the wood stove when the wind blew door doors wide open at the same time. It scared the livin' hell out of me! I jumped up buck naked, ready for a fight! But it was just that cold wind blowing through the cabin. I nearly froze to death before I could get both doors closed.

Well, I learned to take pretty good care of myself for those forty days. Cooking was the hardest thing for me. We didn't have no refrigerator, and all I had was flour, beans, potatoes, and all kinds of dried fruit. All of them outfits had a lot of dried fruit in them days. It came in those twenty-five-pound boxes. Most cow outfits also had plenty of canned corn and canned tomatoes. But at my uncle's, there wasn't much for canned food. So, I learned to cook and love beans.

To this day, I still love beans.

Eventually, my uncle came back. He had leased another ranch way up north and we had totake a bunch of cattle up there. Along the way, we stopped about noon. I was riding an old horse named Baby Doll. There was another old boy working with us by the name of J.J. He was a lot older than I was and a damn good bronc rider. He thought he'd make a bronc rider out of me. So,we were out there on day herd, just J.J. and me. The rest had gone to the wagon to eat.

He said, "Let me put a rope in that old horse's flank (Baby Doll) and see what he'll do."

I said, "Alright, let's do it."

He got off his horse and tied a rope on my horse's flank by tying it to the back strings of my saddle and bringing it back out between my horse's hind legs. Then he jerked the rope. Let me tell you! That old horse, boy, he bucked and farted and snorted! He damn near bucked me off. I was yellin'

"Turn that durn rope loose!" But he wouldn't do it. Old J.J. thought that was the funniest thing he ever saw. He'd drop the rope and about the time I'd relaxed, he'd jerk on that damn rope again and away we'd go. But I'll tell you what, that Baby Doll never got loose of me!

A YOUNG COWBOY IN TEXAS

I quit my uncle's outfit early in the summer, and this old kid thought we'd take off for Arizona on horseback. Well, we didn't make it to Arizona that summer, but that's when I went to work for the S.M.S. outfit. We were up there near Spur, Texas, when we ran into this old guy. He told us he had bought a bunch of brood mares he needed to take to Littlefield, way up on the plains. He said, "How about you two guys take 'em up there for me?"

He told us he'd pay us. I don't remember how much it was now, but it damn sure was more than we had in our pockets at the time. Arizona would have to wait. Anyway, we rode our own horses and drove them mares. After we got 'em up there, we halter broke all the old mares and broke all the young ones to ride. Well, this old guy sold them to the S.M.S. outfit. After that we went back and brought another bunch of horses and we worked and broke them horses for him, too.

See, this S.M.S. outfit had about five hundred head of stock mares themselves. I think it was about two hundred fifty they bought from us the first time, and about a hundred the next time. I kind of got acquainted with that outfit during this time–the boss and boys. So, when we delivered the last of the horses, it was gettin' pretty late in the fall, and we decided we'd better head home. We went by the Spur outfit, where all the S.M.S. raised their horses.

I stopped and said to this old kid, "You go home if you want, but I'm going to stay up here." That's when I went to work for the S.M.S. Ranch. That was the fall of 1928. I was seventeen years old.

They started me out with thirty-five dollars a month and board. That winter, I stayed in theSpur bunkhouse. The wagon started in spring, sometime in March, I guess. I went in the wagon. That was really the beginning of my career as a cowboy.

The first time with the wagon, we stayed out 'till just before Christmas. We ate our meals at the wagon, slept on the ground in our bedrolls, and took our baths in a stock tank. You could go to town in that outfit pretty often. In each camp, they would have an old pickup or something. The S.M.S. outfit owned about three more big ranches besides the Spur. Going way back, the S.M.S. had been the Spur Ranch at one time. They branded the Spur. The Spur Ranch owned the town and all the country around. The town was called Spur. Later on, the S.M.S. bought them out and branded S.M.S. They raised a lot of good horses.

Well, we broke all of them horses. We broke two, three and four-year-old colts every spring. Four of us would take turns in the bronc pen. After we got a horse where you could drag him out and saddle him up, and if somebody could get up on him—well, why then, that horse was broke. It didn't matter how long we could stay on their backs. Once they were ridden, they were broken.

One time, all the spring colts were broke. The Spur Ranch got first pick. They'd send the rest on to the other three outfits. One was at Stamford, one was at Flattop, and one was at Tongue River. I was never on any of those ranches.

I had a lot of good buds in those days. Most everybody, I worked with were good friends. Oh, I did have a run-in or two there with this Texas boy. This one feller, Donny, was kind of short and heavy. Well, I called him "Shorty" one mornin.' I was only about eighteen years old, just a skinny kid.

Donny said, "Well, I ain't too short to whip your skinny ass."

I said, "I think you are."

So, we went at it. I whipped him alright, mostly 'cause he had a hard time reaching me. He did manage to land a few good blows before it was over, though. We became the very best of friends after that. I will never forget him. He finally ended up marrin' a cousin of mine.

Looking back, I guess I was lucky I never got hurt real bad when I was young–not like some guys. Oh, I guess I had a few broken ribs and general cuts and bruises. But nothin' I would call bad, nothing I didn't recover from. Though, I did have a lot of trouble with my ankle and foot for a while after a horse rolled over on it. And I did break my ribs and my collarbone that time. But I've never had no leg bones or arm bones broken.

LEAVING TEXAS

In the winter of 1931, I was camped in a teepee tent. (Similar to a high-walled canvas tent but modeled after a teepee.) It was snowing and cold, and the wind blew like hell. This old boy I knew pretty well named Bill Weatherby came by one day.

He said, "Hey Joe, I'm goin' to head for Arizona as soon as I can. Why don't you go with me?"

What happened was, he had got a couple local girls knocked up, and he decided he best make himself scarce! Well, I asked him about the country in Arizona.

He said, "It's real nice country. The wind never blows and it's never cold. I'm going to be leavin' out soon."

I said, "Well, let me know and I'll go with you."

I was only about twenty years old then. Well, he came by one evening and said, "I'm 'bout ready to go. Move your stuff into the ranch and come on up to our place."

His folks lived near Rotan, so I went to see my momma and folks. I also took all my stuff to keep there. Then I packed up two horses, said my goodbyes, and rode up to his place. This all took about four or five days, and then we were ready to go. I took my horses down to the lower end of his folk's place and turned them out.

We headed for Arizona in an old 1921 Chevy, touring car of some kind. The top was tornup, and no good to us, and the door on the passenger side was missing. I have no idea where old Bill got the thing. We had about twenty flats a day on them. Old, rough, rocky roads. We drove that old thing through Amarillo, Albuquerque, Gallup, Holbrook, and Winslow and attracted lotsof attention. We made quite a show.

We camped along the road most of the time, but once, we did get a room in Gallup and hung out there for a few days. Bill liked to hit the bars and talk to pretty girls. After we got to Flagstaff, we stayed around there for a few days. I don't know why, but my friend Bill decided to go to California. I guess he just needed to get more miles between him and Texas.

I knew an old boy I had worked with in Texas who was working at the CO Bar. He told me quite a bit about the outfit. So, when Bill got ready to go on to California, I said, "Well, I think I'll quit you here."
I had little money, so I gave him twenty bucks. All I had with me at the time was a bedroll and saddle.

Joe 1983

ARIZONA

There was an old auto court on Route 66 owned by a man named Brooks, right there on the north side of the underpass as you get into Flag. I took a room there and gave the guy enough money to stay a couple of weeks. I hung around town talkin' to folks about findin' work and meetin' people. After my friend pulled out for California, I went up to the CO Bar office. Bygolly, within a week or so, I went right to work.

One of them Babbit boys, I can't remember which one, came and got me in an old truck and hauled me out to the Cedar Ranch. That's where the wagon was at the time, and I went with the wagon. Hell, I think we moved out that afternoon. We went to the SF Ranch, where we had a bunch of yearlings to take to the Spider Web Ranch.

I made a lot of friends in that outfit. Old Skeet Black, Percey Wolf, and Ray Ely were all my buds. The old boy who was the cook was named Buck something. Charlie Young was the foreman. That's what we called the managers in those days, anyway. He took care of all the cattle and us cowpunchers. He also was in charge of sellin' the cattle for the ranch.

It was pretty early, in the spring of 1931, when I went to work there. An old boy had just quit, and I was supposed to get his winter horses.

Instead, they ran two in on me that hadn't even been "started" (trained). They were colts, oh, about four or five-year-olds–big horses. Oh, I had a hell of a time with them two horses. But I had one real gentle horse, so I started those two colts myself.

I was with the wagon probably up 'till June. We moved a bunch of yearlings to the Spider Web. Then we took about five hundred head of cattle to Buckler Ranch south of the Grand Canyon. Then we moved them over to Anita on the railroad (The Grand Canyon Railroad).

At Anita, we rounded up all their grass horses–horses that had been livin' in those big grassy parks up there all summer. We each had about ten or fifteen of them horses to work and break. When we were done with that, we got busy cuttin' the yearlings from the cows and weaning the calves. Eventually, we moved back up to the Spider Web and did the same thing there.

While we were at the Spider Web, the cowboy working cows on the Little Colorado River quit. His name was Wesley Banks. There was another old boy staying there to run thewater pumps. The foreman said he needed to send someone down on the river that knew something about a river.

Ol' Charlie Young said to me, "Did you ever work on a river?"I said, "Hell, I was raised on two of 'em."

He said, "Alright, pack up two of your best horses and head for the river."

So, I packed up my two best horses. They were young horses, just colts, really the same two I started with that had given me so many problems. Well, I started on down to the river. In the meantime, they had moved five thousand head of cattle down there 'cause they had no water anywhere else. There were three or four wells up and down the river. The old man that was livin' there at the time--all he did was maintain the pumps, cut wood, and do the cookin' for the cabin. I stayed up there 'till August. It was late into August that year before it ever went rainin.'

The cabin we stayed at was just a little red house right near Black Falls on the Little Colorado. Right below Wupatki was a spring called Heiser Springs, located in a canyon. That canyon ran plum down to the Little Colorado and emptied out just below Black Falls. Generally, that's where our cows were–right there between Black Falls and Cameron. I'm pretty sure that the old house is still there. When you leave Spider Web Ranch, you can go straight east over that black mesa, or you can go around it. There was a big pasture at that black mesa that was fenced in plum to the Little Colorado River. You could go around the mesa and go by a cement tank in a big box canyon. There was an old wagon road that went on east to the house from there.

I rode this country a lot between the Spider Web and the cabin. One evening, it was gettin' kind of dark–whenever you left Spider Web camp, or any camp out there for that matter, you never got back 'till after dark. I was ridin' up an old Indian wagon road towards Heiser Springs, when out in some bushes, a good-looking piece of canvas caught my eye. I wondered why in the hell that canvas was there. It was real spooky lookin,' and my horse was actin' real funny. He was rollin' his eyes and snortin.' Well, I got down off my horse and hung on to the reins and kind of eased over to the canvas. I reached down and slowly raised the canvas, and shit, there was a dead Indian under it! Well, I let out a yelp and jumped straight up into the air. About that time, my horse let out a scream and started dragging me by the reins. Once I got the horse calmed down, I tied him to a bush and went back for a closer look. I raised the canvas again, this time so I could see his face. And I'll be damned, but that old boy was shot right between the eyes! It looked to me like he'd only been dead a couple of hours. Boy, I dropped the canvas, jumped on my pony, and got the hell out of there! Well, I never told nobody about it, and never heard anything about it after that.

There was an old Mexican sheepherder there at Heiser Spring, and his job was to keep the Navajos and their livestock away from the water. His name was Ramon. I used to go by there and eat with him every time I rode through there. He'd always have a good pot of beans and some fresh corn tortillas handy. But I couldn't help but wonder if it was him who shot that poor Indian for some reason or other. Guess I'll never know.

By late August, the rains finally came–and they came hard! The river got high fast. Alongthat river, there's a lot of quicksand. I spent a lot of time that year boggin' livestock out of quicksand. A lot of cowboys would just throw a loop over the critter's heads, then dally the rope around the saddle horn and start pullin.' I seen a lot of critters killed that way. A horse's neck will break pretty easy. A cow can be pulled by the horns, but if you try to pull a cow out of a bog by her tail, you'll pull it right off. A horse or a cow might break a leg if you only get the frontlegs out. They start floundering around and break their hind legs that are still stuck in the mud. I mostly had to get off my horse and wade out into the mud and try and loosen the cow's legs a little. Then, I would put my rope around the body, just behind the front legs. Once I climbed back on my horse, all I had to do was pull. You always wanted to pull straight in line with the rest of the body to keep from snapping a leg. I was always wet and muddy during that time, and I ruined a good pair of boots. Sometimes, I would just strip down to my underwear to keep my clothes dry. That was awful hard work.

After the summer rains came, old Charlie, the foreman, came and got the cattle and me from the river. Then I went back with the wagon. We started around the works again, brandin' the calves and scatterin' the cattle. We'd take a bunch to the Buckler Ranch, then on to the Redlands Ranch. Then we'd go back to the Cedar Ranch and start all over again. At Redlands, we started brandin' spring calves. We branded calves all the way around. We went to Cedar Ranch and branded calves, to Buck's tank and branded calves, to Spider Web and branded calves, then on to the SP. There was a bunch of cattle down there, so we branded those calves, too, before we headed back to the railroad at Anita.

Anita is where we would usually take the cattle for shipping. A man named Cliff Banks was always camped there for the CO Bar. After we got all those cows to Anita, they just left me and another old cowboy, Ed Gore, there. We cut our horses out of the remuda, and the wagon left us. They told us to run all the wild horses and break 'em as we caught 'em.

We stayed there at Anita camp. The trains were still runnin' regular then. Well, we started runnin' all the wild horses in the area. They had given us two or three gentle mules to "neck" the broncs with when we caught 'em. When we found some wild horses, the three of us, me, Clint, and Ed, we would try to drive 'em into a water lot–a fenced-in water tank. If we couldn't drive 'em, we roped 'em anywhere we could. Each day, we took all our saddle horses with us so if we had any broncs in the water lot, we could run our horses in with 'em. We'd never catch any broncs we figured weren't worth breaking. At the end of the day, we'd just turn 'em out and start with another bunch somewhere else in the morning.

After we roped a bronc, we'd tie 'em down. Then we'd catch one of the gentle mules and "neck" 'em–just tie 'em to the mules's halter. Then we'd drive these mules with the Broncs back to camp. We'd start ridin' them broncs right there in the holding pens at Anita. If we didn't have time that evening, we'd just lay off a day or two–rest up before we'd start ridin' broncs again.

After ridin' in the pens, we'd take 'em back out and run the piss heads out. There were a lot of dog holes (prairie dogs) in that country, and while we were runnin' 'em, it was nothin' for one of 'em to step in a dog hole and fall down. If one ever fell down, he'd just get up and go off with the rest of the wild horses. Usually, a couple of guys on saddle horses would find 'em and catch 'em somewhere and bring 'em back to us.

There was a section foreman and crew livin' there with us cowboys. At that time, there was a bunch of houses strung up and down the ridge west of the railroad in Anita. There was also a family living there in those days. The old boy's name was Les Cram. He had two or three daughters, and they had their own house there. One of them daughters was about my age and a real good lookin' red headed woman. Me and all the other boys sure kept an eye on her. Her namewas Kelly Cram. I wonder what ever happened to her. Well, we never did nothin' but try and talk to her once in a while. Heck, we were always dirty and stunk all the time like cow shit. I wasn't too comfortable about approaching her. For one thing, when I was growing up, I never was around women. I guess I was half bashful!

Once in a while, there would be a girl raised up on a ranch and she'd get out and help.

She'd usually be in camp with her family. The wagon would move close to camp, and of course, her daddy would work with the wagon. Then, his daughter would come out and ride with us. Usually, she'd just kind of be around. The gals were a lot like we were in that they were never around men. They were always real nice and we were real nice to them. If we hadn't been we might have gotten a wet rope used on us.

Baths were pretty scarce back then. Water was hard to come by and not something to waste. The rail hauled us our water at Anita. The CO Bar had a big cement tank there, and they'd buy a tank load of water at a time. That's where we got water for camp and watering our horses, cows, and dogs. Us cowboys would try to get a bath once or twice a month. I never had a towel ora washrag while I was in camp, but sometimes a bar of soap would show up. Often, all I could dowas wet my old bandana at a stinkin,' off-colored watering hole to scrub my head and neck.

Around the camps, there was always one of them big old washtubs. It was usually some single old boy livin' in those camps, so we'd borrow his washtub and take a bath. This was in the wintertime. In the summertime, we just took baths in the old stock tanks. We'd go in with our clothes and all. Sometimes, if they got too filthy, we'd take 'em off and rinse 'em. In the summer, we also liked to go into one of them dirt tanks almost every night just to cool off. Generally, we were always camped at one of 'em.

Well, I had started the CO Bar in the spring, but it was gettin' late fall by now. So, we started all over again. Working all over the country and shipping all the old cows and big calves we had weaned that spring. When we started moving cattle to the railroad, we were all so spread out when they started up another chuck wagon. Lee Young ran one wagon, and Tom More was runnin' the other wagon. We would get the cattle rounded up and take 'em to the railroad to be shipped. Then we'd go back to wherever the next bunch was, pick them up and take them to the railroad. By the time we got the last bunch to the railway, it was pretty late in the fall and had turned durned cold. The wet, blowin' snow never seemed to quit. I remember old Bill swore up and down before we left for Arizona that the wind never blew, and it was never cold. That's about the time I quit.

About that time, I got a letter from an old boy back in Texas offering me a chance to runan outfit. So, that's what I did. I went back to Texas and ran that outfit 'till the next spring. It worked out for a while, but it was a family affair, and they got to fightin' and squabblin' with each other, so I quit. This was just a small outfit up in the Panhandle of Texas. I stayed through the winter, then headed back for Arizona. This was the spring of 1932. I rode the Santa Fe railroad from Amarillo to Flagstaff. Just a couple of days after I came back to Arizona, I went to work for the 3V's Ranch in Seligman. I worked there 'till I guess we'd made a full round of brandin' calves and weanin' yearlings.

I remember when I was working at the 3Vs, we'd sometimes go

into Seligman. There wasn't much there, so we'd end up in Ashfork or Williams–usually Williams. We'd go in a big truck, and they'd drop us off, then send the truck back to get us a couple of days later.

Old Russ Perner was the general manager at the 3V's while I was workin' there. One time early in the fall, old Perner came out to the wagon and said to us, "Tomorrow is election day. I'll let you guys all go to town if you all vote and vote the way I want you to."
We all said, "Sure, we'd vote the way he wanted us to."

He took us to Williams in a big old truck, and we all got rooms in some of the roomin' houses there. 'Course, we all got drunker than hell first thing. Well, he said we could stay overnight. Some of us did vote, but we voted however we wanted. Most of 'em got too drunk to vote anyway. I remember that was the year Franklin D. Roosevelt was elected, and I voted for him.

The next day, old Perner sent out a truck to get us, but none of us would go back to the wagon. We were just havin' too much fun! We told the driver, "hell, we ain't done yet!" So, the driver went back to Seligman and told Perner. That truck came for us three days in a row, and still, we wouldn't go back with him.

Finally, on the fourth day, we were so broke and pooped out we just had to go back with him. Hell, he couldn't afford to can us 'cause we were a good crew. It was branding season, and we were riding a lot of young horses. He pretended he was mad, but I knew he really didn't give a damn.

That was the only time I ever voted in my life until I met Dolly. I never cared about that stuff–still don't. I figure they're all crooks. Not once, whoever was president, ever made a difference in my life. Now and then, I might watch it on TV, but I don't care much about it. A lot of cowpunchers never voted in their life. All they ever wanted was to be a cowboy. I was like the rest of those knot-heads. Once I married Dolly, she always made me vote. And she made damn sure it was always for a Republican in the spring of 1934. I quit the 3V's and went back to work for the CO Bar. I was with the wagon for quite a while, and we had practically made the whole round of branding calves. About this time, they sent me with a whole bunch of cattle to the Buckler Ranch to camp there. I camped there a long time 'till they came by to move the cows that were in the forest. (Kaibab National Forest grazing allotment)

We were moving them back to Anita. This was late summer, and the monsoons were heavy that year. It was rainin' like hell! By the time we got into the Red Buttes area, just about ten miles from Anita, we were in a hell of a storm. They bogged the chuck wagon down in the mud, and we had to pull it out with our saddle horses.

Red Buttes was Burt Babbitt's homestead, and there was a big pasture there. Burt Babbitt had a lot of sheep. A cowpuncher did not fool with sheep. The sheepmen had their own separate outfits. We must have had about six or seven hundred head of cows and calves. So, we decided to stay there at Red Buttes two or three days to let the ground dry out.

That night first, there was a hell of a storm–lighting and everything. It was awful.

The sky got blacker, and there was thunder rumblin' all around us. Each time there was a strike of lightning, I would count the seconds before the thunder rolled. It was coming towards us. It got so black it was like night. The only times I could see any of the other cowboys was when there was a blue glow from a lightning bolt. The lightning hit somewhere close, and I could see it coming across the cow's horns. It was jumping from one horn to the next. That was the first time I ever saw what they call St. Elmo's fire. I was ridin' on point, and somebody else was on the other point. I was ridin' a great big white horse when a bolt of lightning went right by me! I would swear that lightning went right down that horse's shoulder. After it went past me, it hit a big cedar tree not a hundred feet from me. It just tore that cedar all to hell! My horse didn't react too much 'cause all the horses were pretty much used to lightning. But I'm sure they were all scared, though. I know all the cowpunchers were scared to death. That was a hard night on all us cowpunchers. We were scared the cattle would stampede, but they never did.

It was that same summer I was ridin' alone, gathering cattle west of Anita. It was a cool, cloudy summer day. There was a lot of dry lightning going on around the area when a bolt came down and killed my horse right from under me. It seemed like the bolt hit the ground right in front of us and somehow killed my horse instantly. Well, the blast had knocked me out, and I don't remember anything for a while. But when I come to, I and my dead horse were layin' there on the ground. I wasn't hurt bad, but that damn horse was layin' on my left leg, and I couldn't get loose. I tried diggin,' but it was all rocky and I couldn't dig with my bare hands. I was pretty scared by then. I laid there for ten or twelve hours–pretty sure I was going to die.

It was good and dark when I heard leather creakin' and a horse walkin.' I hollered out and along came Clint Banks. He had got worried about me and tracked me down. I was sure glad to see him. He used his horse to lift the dead horse up enough for me to pull my leg out. It was sore as hell and bruised bad, but not broke. We pulled my saddle and gear off the dead horse and hid it in the brush to come back for. I rode back to camp behind Clint. I wasn't hurt bad, but I was sure hungry!

Come fall, the ranch put me to helpin' the fencin' crew. Each ranch had their own fencin' crew that did nothin' but build fences. They had another outfit that 'tanked.' That means they did nothin' but build water tanks and clean out water tanks. In those days, it was all done by horse and mule teams. Everything was done on horseback. They camped wherever they were workin.' Fence buildin' was really hard work in those days. They had to cut the posts and dig the holes–no iron posts in those days. Some of the fence builders were old-time cowpunchers that couldn't get a job ridin' anymore or just thought fence buildin' was an easier job. There was always one old guy who would be the foreman of the fencin' crew. He usually had an old truck he'd use to haul supplies out to the fence builders. If they run out of groceries or hay or grain for their teams, the foreman would go into Flag, then haul all the supplies out to the crew-- wherever they were camped. Then he'd stay there in camp with us 'till he had something else to do. He and his crew also hauled firewood out to the cow camps. In a lot of the cow camps, there was no firewood–especially around the Spider Web. He and his crew would go on up the side of the peaks (San Francisco Peaks) and cut wood. Anywhere he could use his truck, he'd use it. He'd haul groceries and hay and grain out to us cowboys. 'Course, in the summertime, we didn't need any grain or hay. We just rode grass horses.

Well, a couple of weeks of that was all I could take. So, I told old C.J. Babbitt I was goin' to quit. He talked me out of it by letting me go back with the wagon. Old C.J. wasn't a bad guy. But I didn't talk to the Babbitt family very much. Although, I used to talk to young Johnny Babbitt once in a while, he was a real nice man. He was always in school and never punched cows but came out during the summer to fool around a bit. Johnny was the only Babbitt I got to know well enough to like. 'Course C.J. was the general manager, and us cowpunchers never did get to know the managers all that good.

  I was sure glad to get back to the wagon that fall. When we were with the wagon, we always ate good. We always had a lot of fun at the roundups with the wagons along. The boys were always jokin' and horsin' around in the evenings. 'Course, we didn't play too late 'cause we had to get up damn early in the morning, usually around three or four o'clock. It wasn't hard to get up 'cause you would hear the clatterin' and bangin' of Dutch ovens and pots and pans. The cook always woke the wrangler up first to help get the cookin' fires going. Boy, I tell ya, there was nothing like waking up layin' there in your bedroll in the crisp mountain air, smellin' the hot biscuits in the Dutch ovens and a big pot of hot coffee boilin' away. I sure did love that. Hey, did you ever hear the cook's mornin' grub call?

"Get up, Joe, the day's a breakin,' coffee's a cookin,' and biscuits a bakin.'Roll out, cowboy, come and get it.
Get 'er while she's hot, or we'll throw her out and spit in the skillet."
Every outfit also had a guy who wrangled horses. A cowpuncher never had to wrangle horses or fool with the cookin.' There was always a wrangler whose job it was to take care of the horses. During the day, he'd take 'em out where they could graze. He'd watch over 'em 'till we'd come in at night. Once we come in, usually ten or twelve of us, a couple of us would go out and relieve the wrangler so he can come in and eat. While we were there, we would tie up the horses we were going to ride the next day. There was generally a horse pasture within a mile or two.

After the wrangler had his supper, he would take all the horses and put 'em in the pasture overnight. The next morning, he'd take 'em out and graze 'em again. Every day was just the same old thing for the horse wrangler.

I remember the horse wrangler at the 3V's was named John Daley. The old boy that wrangled horses at the CO Bar were Steve something. I forgot his last name. It was kind of a whoop name. He went nuts one night and started shooting an old twenty-two rifle at everybody. He never hit anybody, and I don't think he was trying to. All us cowpunchers high-tailed it out into the rocks 'till he calmed down. He was yellin' he was going to kill himself. Most of us stayed hid the rest of the night. The next morning, they had to take him away. The next old boy they hired was the same guy who had quit down on the Little Colorado River, Old Wesley Banks.

Generally, at these camps, we were all alone. Sometimes, some old guy would be sent into town to buy a whole supply of groceries, including everything we needed: flour, beans, meat, bacon–no fresh meat–but all kinds of dried fruit. Anytime one of us cowpunchers had to go out to camp alone, they'd haul us each a load of groceries. Everything they brought was in cases. We ate good. When we were out alone, we couldn't butcher beef, and it wouldn't keep anyway–especially in the summertime. But the wagon always had fresh beef. If the wagon was anywhere around close, they'd send us a quarter of beef. They butchered a cow almost every day with the wagon.

You know, most of the time, cowboys are gentlemen with good manners. The main reason is, damn, around those chuck wagons on the big outfits, they would teach you to have good manners. Those damn cooks, they'd hang a poker on your neck if you didn't watch out. You had to watch what you said, and you had to watch your manners while eatin' around the wagon.

First, you went to the chuck box and got your dishes. Then you went to the Dutch ovens and got your grub. Your bedroll was always rolled up somewhere close by, so you'd take your plate and coffee and go sit on your bedroll. Generally, a couple of old boys would sit on the same bedroll and talk. When we were done, there was a big dishpan called a "wreck-pan" full of hot water under the mess-box lid. Each cowboy had to rinse his dirty dishes out in the wreck pan and stack 'em neatly for the cook or wrangler to wash 'em good later.

You'd really have to watch yourself when you were eatin.' Them damn cooks were really rank. I never saw one that wasn't! After you got your plate, you did not walk between the Dutch ovens and the chuck box because it was always dusty. You had to really watch what you did around the wagons. One thing, you never rode your horse through the "kitchen," and you always made sure to ride downwind of the wagon, so you did not get dust in the food. The cook was the boss around the wagon. Why, it wasn't surprising at all for a cook to get pissed off and whip a cowpuncher with his own chaps. He'd get a couple cowboys to hold the poor feller down and whip him good. I seen it happen more than once!

When you were outside and away from the chuck wagon, you could say or do whatever you wanted. The food was always good. But if you didn't like what was cooked that day, you sure never said nothin' to the cook. If a cowboy complained about the cook's food, the pissed-off cook would start doin' stuff like put salt in your coffee or make your helpin's short. I've seen cooks flat-out refuse to feed a cowboy who complained about his cooking. But if everybody was nice to the old cook, we might get a special treat at supper time, like peach cobbler or "spotted pup pudding."

Most of the time, the wagon food was delicious and plentiful. Beef and beans were mostly what we had. There was almost always a pot of "whistle berries" at supper time. My favorite was the fried steak, pan gravy, and hot bakin' biscuits. The cook would slice off a bunch of thick steaks and pound 'em with a hammer to make 'em good and tender. Once the Dutch ovens were hot, he'd throw in a big handful of fat suet off the same beef. The fat melted and was sizzlin' hot, about an inch deep. Each steak was salted and dipped in flour before thrown into the hot grease. After the steaks were done just right–in those days a cowboy always wanted his steak well done–the cook would make pan gravy to sop our biscuits in. Man, it was good! Only city slickers liked their meat broiled rare. Broiling loses all the juices and fat. I heard about a cowboy in a town restaurant tell the waitress that his steak was too rare. He said, "My god, I seen cow's git well that was hurt worse than this!"

Breakfast was usually fried sow belly with biscuits. We'd take an extra biscuit and some bacon and stuff it in our pockets for lunch. Sometimes, we'd get pancakes for breakfast, sweetened with molasses. We never had eggs 'cause we couldn't keep 'em fresh.

You know, the cook was usually an old-time cowboy who was able to handle horses, drive a wagon and cook. I know for a fact most old-time cooks made more money than us cowpunchers.

We'd go to town about twice a year for Christmas and the Fourth of July—usually, Williams or Flag. The only time a real cowboy drank was when he went to town. There were only two things to do when you went to town. First, we'd get cleaned up and get a haircut. Then we'd get drunker than hell and go visit one of those cat houses. When we were in Flagstaff, we stayed at the Monte Vista or the Weatherford Hotel. About that time, my only experience with women was with them whores in Flagstaff or Williams. They were usually very nice to us cowboys, and some of them was durn pretty. We'd sometimes take them down to Weatherford to get a meal or just take them for a walk around. There were plenty of bars along Highway 66 in Flagstaff at that time. I liked women; I just didn't have time for 'em. I always said I'd never get married. I had three or four uncles that never did get married. Hell, a cowpuncher shouldn't get married. There was just no place for a wife. Besides, the type of gals you met when you came to town, you sure didn't want for a wife.

    Well, that's all a dumb cowboy knew to do in town. They'd let us stay there three or four days before they'd gather us up and haul us back to the wagon. Sure, we'd buy a few things for ourselves. I always bought my own Bull Durham and a new pair of Levi's. That's all I ever needed from town. At the time, I was making sixty dollars a month, and they furnished everything else I needed.

    In 1937, I quit the CO Bar. I went to work down in the Sedona area for old Clay Lockett. I broke a bunch of horses for him that year. I was working for him when I got hurt real bad. That time, I thought I was going to lose my mind. A horse fell on me and damn near broke my neck and back. He had a whole bunch of broncs for me to ride that summer. This one horse was a real nice-lookin' colt, but he bucked like hell. If you were outside the corral and get him to lopin' or runnin,' well, he'd break in two. He'd buck and snort. He'd kick so high behind that he'd almost kick your legs off. Me being, so long-legged, I'd have to get my feet way on top of his neck to keep from being kicked. This old horse got so high that he just turned upside-down, and I was the first thing that hit the ground, with him landing on top of me.

I was camped there at Harris Park, just me and Bill Sullivan. He was just a kid, maybe fourteen or fifteen. I had no way to get to a hospital. We were all alone that summer and I was hurt bad. I couldn't do anything there for a couple of weeks in camp. Finally, old Lockett, who had been in Wyoming, came out to camp. I told him I was hurt bad and was going to quit, so he hauled me into Flag. I could hardly move, but he helped me on the Greyhound bus. I wanted to go back to Texas and see my momma. I was scared and thought something bad was going to happen to me.

Texas was real dry that winter, there wasn't much grass. The outfit I had worked for before had a whole bunch of cows in the feed lot there in Rotan. I fed those cows in that feed lot all winter. When the cows left in the spring I was feeling better. So, I packed up and left for Arizona.

I went to work for the DK outfit at Rodger's Dry Lake Ranch in the fall of 1938. They were shippin' cattle out of there then. The Millers owned the Windmill Ranch in the Verde Valley and the DK at Rodger's Lake. They had grazing permits from the Verde Valley to Bellmont. Oh, the good thing about DK Ranch was that it was pretty close to the railroad siding at Bellmont. We drove the cattle to Bellmont for shipping. But in 1942, the Army took over the area and built the Navajo Army Depot. So, the railroad built a spur out there near Riordan, just east of Bellmont.

We'd drive the cattle right over there from Rodger's Lake to load 'em on the railroad cars. That went on for some years 'till the railroad did away with the Riordan siding for some reason. After that, we started haulin' 'em all out by trucks in the fall. The Williams Grand Canyon Railroad was a little too far for our fall drives. Anyway, that's almost all CO Bar country anyway–all the way north to the Park (Grand Canyon). There was another ranch up in that country owned by Bob Thurston. His outfit also used the Grand Canyon Railroad. Thurston's ranch stretched west of the Grand Canyon Village to the Hualapai Reservation.

In 1942, when the war had started, I was working for the DK. I was only thirty-one years old, and I figured I was going to have to join the Army. There was an old boy in Prescott wanting me to go there and drive a 'cat' (bulldozer) for him. His name was Charlie Weston, and he lived just outside Prescott, with three or four sections of land and a few cattle. That fall, I was breaking horses for the DK there at Frye Park. I was camped right there where that old log cabin was. Old Charlie was building a big tank there on the flat at Frye Park. He came to me one day and said, "I need a cat-skinner (bulldozer operator). If you ever get some time, come on down, and I'll teach you to drive a cat."

I figured I was going into the Army soon anyway. So, after I got my colts started pretty good, I took a couple of days off, then headed down there to drive a cat. Charlie paid pretty good money. I can't remember how much now, but it was a lot more than what I made punchin' cows. As a cowpuncher, I think I was making seventy-five dollars a month. Anyway, Charlie and I got to be real good friends. I drove the cat for him some, built some fences, and helped out with his cattle. By then, I had my draft notice. So, I went to the Army recruiting office in Phoenix and took my physical. And I'll be damned if they didn't turn me down. I had a rupture. Hell, I never knew it! I was kinda disappointed because I felt like I should be over there in the war with the mother boys. I tried to know a little something that was going on with the war 'cause I took that Life Magazine. I didn't get a whole lot of news. Sometimes, there would be an old radio on the wagon or at one of the camps to listen to.

After I knew I wasn't going into the Army, I quit Charlie Weston. I just didn't want to drive a cat anymore. I ran around for a while and went back to Seligman to look around. I didn't see anything there that I wanted. I had a chance to go to work for the 3V's again, but I just didn't want to.

I ended up wranglin' dudes at the Grand Canyon. Them dudes was sure a handful. They couldn't do a damn thing for themselves. I sure hated that job. Oh, every once in a while, I got to talkin' to a pretty girl and that was okay. But most of them people were sure hard to like. I had been working there only about two weeks when a train load of new bronc mules came in there atthe Grand Canyon Village. They said to me. "How would you like to like to move out to Yaqui camp and break these mules?"

I said, "Sure."

So, they sent me and Charlie Vespers out to Yaqui Point to break mules and pack supplies down to Phantom Ranch. We broke them mules, got 'em where we could pack 'em and ride 'em.
Packin' supplies down to Phantom was alright; there was no one looking over our shoulder. They'd put us up in the little bunkhouse they had down there. There was a little café where they fed us supper. Sometimes, we'd take a dip in the swimming pool they had built for the dudes. That water was the coldest water I ever swam in. But it sure felt nice on a good, hot

summer evening. Then, for some reason, Charlie quit. After he quit, I didn't want to stay--so I quit, too.

About that time, the Forest Service (Coconino National Forest) was buildin' a lot of fences and fixin' old ones. I was hired on to help. I strung a lot of wire and spent a lot of time ridin' and fixin' fence. I would usually drag a horse in a trailer out to a starting point somewhere. I'd pack a lunch, usually a can of tomatoes or peaches and maybe some jerked beef. Then I'd get my equipment together. I carried an old canvas sack tied to my saddle. In it would be a good pair of fencin' pliers, the kind with a hammer on one side and wire cutters on the other side. I also carried an old boot-top sewn together at the bottom, this I filled with fence staples and bailing wire. That's about all the tools I needed.

I'd patrol maybe five to ten miles of fence a day, makin' repairs as I went. A lot of things would break a fence in them days. Sometimes, lightning would burn up a post. Sometimes, two bulls would get in a fight and push the staples out of the posts or just snap the wire. One big problem we had was them damn elk jumpin' the fences. If they couldn't clear the top wire, the weight of them elk would snap the wire like a thread. I also spent many a day fixin' a washed-out water-gap or puttin' in a new Texas gate. It was hard work.

About that time, the DK got ready to go back to work for the fall roundup. Old Cecil Miller came to see me and wanted me to come back to work for them. That was the fall of 1947, and I was sure ready to quit the Forest Service and that damn fence ridin'.

They sent me to Phoenix with a whole bunch of those broncs I had been riding before I quit the DK the last time. Some had been ridden since I broke 'em, and some hadn't. I took five heads with me. Cecil had bought a thousand head of cows and put them on the Miller Farm near Phoenix. I spent the winter takin' care of them cows. Old Cecil said if I went to work for him, he's pay for an operation on my rupture. Sure enough, while I was down there in Phoenix that winter, he put me up in the Good Samaritan Hospital and had me operated on.

That spring, after he sold the cattle in Phoenix, Cecil canned his foreman, Paul Moore. He then sent me up to Rodger's Dry Lake to run the damn thing. Because of the war it is was awfulhard to buy groceries and things. Old Doc McCauley and I practically ran the place and did almost all the ranches work ourselves. Until about 1944, we really couldn't get any help 'cause all the young guys were gone to war. Doc was getting old, and I was still recuperating from that rupture operation.

Doc was a hell of a good old boy. He had a homestead near a place they called Grindstone. He always had a few cattle, but he "coyote" 'em– you know, kept them out of sight of the Forest Service. While we worked together, we became the best of friends. He was a damn good cowboy. We were as close as two guys could be. He worked at the DK almost as long as I did. After I left the DK and married Dolly, Doc left too. He did a little bit of everything and began to accumulate a little land here and there. He ended up with a few hundred head of cows.

So, I lived at Rodger's Dry Lake headquarters on and off. Most of the time, I was out in camp. I'd rather go to the camps 'cause there were always too many people at the headquarters in the summertime. I stayed at Winter Cabin in Sycamore Canyon. I stayed at Buck Ridge Cabin and Potato Patch in Barney Pasture. I also stayed at Frye Park a lot. I camped all over around Turkey Butte and Lockwood Springs. I had that water lot there at Flat Tank built. Me and another old boy built the water lot at Coon's Tank. We camped there a lot. I helped build Buck Ridge Cabin sometime in the late 1930's, but it burned down. We built the second one that's there now in 1942. When we were finished, we had a real nice cabin. It had new wood stoves and was very livable.

I don't know who actually did the work on Taylor Cabin, but I do know who had built it. It was a three-way partnership between the B Cross, owned by Ben Perkins, the DK Ranch, owned by the Millers, and Nick Perkins–I forgot his brand.

It was 1938, or '39 that we built that cement dam near there. I packed the cook stove for the cabin in there. I first had to pack one hundred bags of cement for the dam. Once they used all that up, I had to pack fifty more sacks. I also packed in all the lumber. There were two more boys stayin' there at the cabin, and they packed in all the sand. They had a saddle horse and a pack mule apiece. They packed all the sand and rocks out of the creek bed. They must have used a million round rocks out of Sycamore Creek in that cement dam. When they poured the cement, I packed the water they used from the creek. When I was packin' cement, I left my mules at Black Tank at night. I kept an old truck there, so I'd drive back to the Windmill Ranch and spend the night. In the morning, I'd load up my cement and hay and grain if I needed it and head for Taylor Cabin. Those were some long days. Towards springtime, when the rains came, Sycamore Creek got pretty high. I couldn't go everyday then 'cause some of the pack mules were real small and I was afraid I might get the cement wet crossing the creek. I had to cross Sycamore Creek many times to get to Taylor Cabin from Black Tank. Old Bud Jones helped me do some of the packin.' We had twenty head of mules.

One time, me and another old boy were on a wild cow hunt in Sycamore Canyon. There were plenty of mixed cattle of all ages. And there were a lot of steers in Sycamore 'cause it was such rough country they could hide out during the fall roundup. This was probably the winter of 1939 or '40, and I had been staying at Winter Cabin with old Ben Stewart. We decided it was time to spend a couple of days and gather as many of them cows as we could. Anyway, we had acouple of good dogs with us and headed down the Winter Cabin Trail in search of cows. Old Ben had only one leg, but he could ride as well as anybody I knew with two legs. He always carried an old homemade crutch on the back of his saddle. It was his right leg missin' just above the knee. He could brace himself up with the crutch long enough to get his left foot in the stirrup, then toss his stump leg over the saddle. He always rode a good, gentle mare that would stand still for him. Ben claimed he had a good wooden leg, but I never saw it.

Well, we found three or four old cows and a couple still suckin,' unbranded calves right off. Some we roped and just tied to a tree, so they'd be there when we came back by. We then caught a couple of wild steers down in the canyon. After we went up the trail to collect the tie dones, we headed the whole bunch where we figured to pen 'em up in the holding pens at Taylor Cabin.

We spent the night at Taylor Cabin, and the next mornin,' after some coffee and canned peaches, we took out again. I said, 'Let's go up some of those draws in Sycamore Basin.' We figured it was going to be some rough goin' in there, but it was probably a good hidin' spot for those old rangy cows. Well, we went down Sycamore trail for a couple of miles before we turned west up Cedar Creek–up into the canyons.

For a couple of hours, we worked them draws, seeing plenty of tracks, but never a cow. Every now and then, we could hear 'em squealin' and crashing through the brush ahead of us. The dogs were barkin' and raisin' hell out ahead of us. We came out at the head of a deep draw and turned north. Here, the country was gettin' thick with manzanita and cliff rose. The slope was steep and rocky and gettin' steeper. I was followin' Ben across some steep bedrock sandstone when his horse decided it was too steep for her. She tried to whirl around but slipped and fell over on her left side and started slidin' down the hill. Ben had seen it coming and got out of the saddle before the horse hit the rock. Ben and his horse were both slidin' and rollin' downhill through all that thick brush. The horse was screamin,' and sparks were just flyin' off her shoes as she slid down the sandstone ledge. I jumped down off my horse and scrambled after them.

Theywere neither one hurt bad. Ben was all scratched up from the brush and cactus, and his horse had scraped off two of her shoes—but they were both okay. I found Ben's crutch and got him up off the ground. That old boy must have weighed two hundred fifty pounds, even with one leg gone.

After the dust settled, I got to lookin' around where we were, and I saw we were on a ledge above a steep-sided draw. And right there, pretty well hidden by the brush, was the entrance of an old my shaft. Well, I made a torch out of an old pinion knot and went in to explore it. It went maybe thirty or forty feet, and no place was high enough to stand in. We found stuff that I know was old Spanish gear. There were old picks and diggin' stuff and what looked like old lantern parts. There were also pieces of an old burro harness. The pick and shovel looked to be hand forged.

We led our horses to the bottom of the draw, where we found a spring and an old Mexican style grinding mill. Not far from there was a big tailings pile at the edge of the wash. I never went back to that place, but I bet I could still find it.

I spent a lot of time in Sycamore Canyon and Winter Cabin in those days. Most of the time, when I camped at Winter Cabin, I was alone. It had a good corral right below the cabin in an open area. It was a good pole corral about six feet high. It had a "water lane" goin' right through it on down to the creek so the horses could water. Sometimes, I would get to feelin' sorry for 'em bein' in the corral, so I'd take 'em over to that old dry lakebed, Ott Lake. There had at one time been a wild cow corral there and a little pasture joined it.

Winter Cabin was the greatest place I ever stayed. I loved staying there.

In those days, there were a lot of wild cattle in Sycamore. The cabin was in real good shape then. In the fall, we would fill the back half of the cabin with hay and grain. The cabin had an old cookstove, a table and a couple of chairs. There was also a bunk bed against one wall and a cupboard stocked with canned food, coffee, bakin' powder, flour, salt, pepper, and canned milk. There were usually a couple of good Dutch ovens hanging from the rafters and other cookin' stuff. There would always be Saturday Evening Post or Reader's Digest magazines layin' around, and if I was lucky, a roll of toilet paper. There wasn't much to do in the evenings; I'd just go to bed. After I got into camp and fed my horses, and cooked my supper, I would just go to bed. Sometimes I had an old kerosene lamp, or else I'd make a lamp out of a whiskey bottle by filling it with gasoline and puttin' a rag in it. I used a lot of those types of lamps. I always got up in the mornin' before the sun came up. Everything I needed I kept in the cabin, except my saddles and tack, those I left outside just hanging on a corral fence or somethin.'

Doc McCauley and his daddy-built Taylor Cabin for a line shack. In the early days there was a smaller log cabin out in front. They stayed there 'till they got the new cabin built.

One day at Winter Cabin, me an' old Doc shot a bear with my twenty-two pistols. We were camped there and were in the process of hauling hay down to the cabin to stock it up for the winter. We each had a saddle horse and three broncs apiece. We were packin' on them durn broncs. They were some of those buckin' horses the DK used to have. Each trip down, we'd lead three pack horses. Each one's halter was tied to the tail of the horse in front–single file. Each horse would have two bales of hay and a hundred-pound sack of grain swingin' from their pack saddles. I had a bedroll over at Buck Ridge Cabin, and one afternoon, we got tired of packin' hay, so I said, "Let's go over to Buck Ridge and get my bedroll." I always kept two bedrolls. Doc agreed 'cause he was tired of packin' hay, too. I don't remember what Doc was ridin.' But I rode one of the broncs– a big, heavy, gray gelding, and led another horse to pack my bedroll.

I had a little dog and Doc had a dog and, on our way, back to Winter Cabin the dogs jumped an old bear. They ran the bear up a dead pine tree and kept him there. We were about half a mile from the cabin and

Doc said to me, "I sure would like to kill that bear–that's good eatin'". Well, we got our ropes down, and Doc threw a loop over the bear's head.

I said, "What the hell are you goin' to do now, tie up that old bear?"

I tried to rope one of his back legs, but every time I threw my rope, that bear would scramble around the other side of the tree. Finally, I got a good loop on one hind foot and pulled it tight. The whole time that durn bronc was throwing a fit. We both had our ropes dallied to our saddle horns, and we pulled that old bear right out of the tree. About that time, we really had a mess. Here we were--tied to a mad bear. The horses were snorty and boogered up. The dogs were jumping in and out, making everything worse. Finally, I figured the best thing was to get off my bronc. I jumped off with the rope and took a couple of good turns around a pinion snag. We had the bear pretty well stretched out.

I told Doc, "I'll return to the cabin and get my pistol. Keep the dogs here and the bear tied to that tree."

So, I rode back as fast as I could to get my twenty-two pistols. When I got back, Doc shot the bear with it right behind the ear. The bear fell dead, and we let lose our ropes. When we did that, a little dog of mine jumped right on top of that bear, kind of straddled him, and got the bear by the throat.

Well, as it turned out, that old bear wasn't quite dead. He reached up around that dog and pulled him to him. Man did that dog buck and howl! It took another shot to finally kill that bear. While we were butcherin' it, there was an old she-bear down below us aways. Every once in a while, she would charge and get pretty close to us. Her hair was standin' straight up, and she was makin' a sound just like an old hog. I was startin' to get worried 'cause I knew that little twenty-two pistol of mine wouldn't stop a charging bear. Finally, she got tired of the dogs and ran off.

We dressed out that stinky old bear and hauled it down to the cabin. Old Doc cooked up a bunch of it. Doc ate it and what he didn't eat, he gave to the dogs. He cut off a hunk of that bear meat and ate it raw like an old hound dog. Hell, Doc loved it! I tried to eat it, but hell, the more I'd chew, the bigger it would get in my mouth. There was no way in hell I could eat that bear.

After Doc skinned it, it looked just like a human being layin' there. I never hunted much except for something to eat. Oh, we ate some wild game in the early days. I used to really like venison. 'Course, I got kind of burned out on it in those camps. We ate quite a bit of deer meat there for a while. In the wintertime, if it was real cold and I had a chance to shoot a real fat deer, I'd probably get one. It didn't matter to me if it was a buck or a doe. When I was working out at the Spider Web, I'd drop an antelope once in a while.

I really loved antelope meat. Sometimes, one of the boys would kill a young turkey or two for camp. But I wouldn't eat turkey–or any kind of fowl for that matter.

While I was still runnin' the DK and before I married Dolly, I was hired to help make a movie. It was called "Badman and the Angel" (1947). Old John Wayne was the star. I liked John Wayne. The movie was filmed just east of old Lady Thomas's place. The stockman for the outfit was named Bob James and he came to see me one day while I was at the Windmill Ranch. I had some damn good-lookin' horses at that time. Anyway, he told me they had four hundred head of Mexican steers to be unloaded at the railroad in Clarkdale. They had lots of help, but they didn't have anybody who knew the country or how to get them steers from Clarkdale to the movie set. They asked if I would help drive the cattle out, and if they could keep 'em there at the Windmill Ranch in the water lot for a few days.

I helped them drive those steers to the Windmill Ranch and let 'em keep 'em there. They fed those four hundred steers and one hundred bales of hay every day! I saw that. They were small bales in those days, of course. All I had to do was furnish the water, and they paid one hundred dollars a day. Well, by then, I was kind of workin' for them. 'Course I was workin' for old man Miller too. When they got ready to film the movie, they asked me if I'd drive all them steers outto the Apperson place. So, I moved them steers to the Apperson place under them red bluffs and that fenced canyon–they had a grazin' lease, too. They started shootin' pictures right there. I worked for them for two weeks.

There was one scene in that movie where there was supposed to be a cattle stampede. During the stampede, a chuck wagon being pulled by a team of horses was supposed to turn over in a wreck. Well, they tried and tried but couldn't get that wagon to roll over. They came to me and asked if I had any ideas.

I said, "Why don't you just pull it over?"

They thought that was a good idea and asked me to help. So, I tied a big heavy rope up high on that wagon box and dallied it to my saddle horn. I was on a big stout bay that I owned. We got the wagon rollin' and a bunch of cow punchers got all them steers runnin' around us. I was just lopin' alongside the chuck wagon. While everything was runnin' good and the dust was flyin,' I just turned my ol' pony away, and that wagon pulled right over. The driver leaped out of the wagon seat just at the right time.

Them movie people thought that I was just great! If you look real close in that movie, you can see me pullin' that wagon over. 'Course I didn't get any extra money for it.

That's also when I met the actor, Ben Johnson and quite a few others. I sure liked Ben Johnson; he was a real nice man.

I had to drive them four hundred head of steers back to Clark Dale and help load em' on the rail cars. They gave me four head to keep for practicin' my ropin' on. I had to quit anyway 'cause we were getting ready to move the DK cattle to the mountain (Rodger's Dry Lake) that spring.

I also helped with a couple of other cowboy movies. One was called "Wanda Nevada" (1979). They had done some filming out by the ranch (Red Canyon), and I rented them four of my horses. They were also filming up at Lee's Ferry on the Colorado River. I went with 'em as they were payin' me two hundred dollars a day. I hauled my horses up in that same four-horse trailer I have out there now. They had another guy there with some fancy horses the movie outfit had brought out with them from Hollywood, I guess. The star of the movie was Peter Fonda. They had built a wooden bridge across an arroyo. The bridge was only maybe ten or twelve feet long and went over a ten-foot-deep wash. Peter was supposed to ride this horse across that wooden bridge– 'course, it was a stuntman doin' the ridin.' Well, none of them fancy movie horses would cross that bridge. As soon as they stepped on the first planks, the noise would bugger 'em, and they'd just balk.

Well, the director looked at me and asked, "You got a horse that will cross that bridge?"

I said, "Sure, as long as I'm the one ridin' her."

So, they dressed me up in the stuntman's clothes, and I rode that big old gray mare of mine right across the bridge--no problem. I never saw that movie, but I bet I'm in it. I have a buck knife inscribed with "Wanda Nevada" on the blade. They gave me that after the shoot.

We had some hard winters in the early days. One of the worst winters I remember, it was 1945 and '46. This old guy named John was snowed in at Rodger's Dry Lake and his family got word that he was out of supplies. They were all worried about him. So Tony, his nephew, who ran the Verde Grocery in Cottonwood gave me some groceries to pack in to him.

Me and this other old cowboy picked out two big mules and couple of big saddle horses from Windmill Ranch. We packed up and drove up there on the highway in a snowstorm and unloaded there at Riordan. Well, we started from Riordan just before dawn, there on Highway 66 between Flagstaff and Bellmont. There was just enough light to barely see where we were. I knew there was going to be a lot of snow in there.

There's a big wash runnin' south from Rior Dan to just about half a mile from Rodger's Lake. I knew there was going to be a lot of runoffs up there, and the snow might not be so deep. We took our loaded mules and followed the water rightup the wash. The snow was comin' down so hard we couldn't even see each other. We left the water at the top of a small summit, and from there, we had to start breaking the trail. The snow was so deep it was clear up to the breast collars of those big horses. We thought for a while we weren't going to make it. Them big stout horses would break through the crust on top and fall down and wallow in it. Sometimes, we could hold 'em up; other times, they'd just break through. It was a real struggle to get 'em out once they fell through. Them poor animals went through hell. The horses and mules had scraped and cut their legs on the ice and were leavin' a trail of blood. At one time, one of the mules broke through and got bogged down bad. He got to floppin' around and the diamond hitch broke loose and scattered groceries and stuff all over. It took us about an hour to fix that wreck and get everything tied back down.

There were many times I was ready to drop the loads and get the hell out of there. My feet and hands were damn near frozen. The other boy was in worse shape. I didn't think he was goin'to make it. But about two in the afternoon, six hours after startin' out, we spotted chimney smoke comin' from the cabin at Rodger's Lake. I don't think I was ever so glad to see that old house.

When we finally pulled up there and got everything untied, we found out that old fool wasn't out of food; he was just lonesome! He'd been snowed in all winter, but all had kinds of groceries! It was pretty late when we got there, about three o'clock, when he fed us. That old fart wanted us to spend the night. But hell no, we'd already had enough bullshit.

After we unpacked and ate, it was time to head out. We were afraid it was going to get dark on us before we got back–which it did. But now the mules were unloaded, and we were following the trail we broke earlier. I didn't get back 'till way after midnight.

It was around 1948 that I bought a small outfit northeast of Kingman. I kept a bunch of cattle there, but mostly, I was still running the DK. It was then I met Dolly. Dolly owned Red Canyon Ranch. Her name was Ehva Pifer, and she was born in 1903 in Michigan. Her folks were Thomas and Grace Oates. I guess Dolly–she always went by Dolly–was married to some old boy named Pifer. He was older than her and died of a heart attack in the early '30s. They owned a trading post in Globe. That's where Dolly got all them Navajo Rugs and baskets. Oh, Dolly could never have kids, we never did have kids.

That first winter, we were married, and we moved into Red Canyon Ranch. It was 1948, and it had snowed four feet. I was still working for the DK. We had to feed the cows at the Windmill Ranch, and we had a lot of cattle in Sycamore Canyon with winter calves. Old Doc McCauley and I decided we'd better go up and check those cattle at Taylor Cabin. We thought there might be some cattle hung up on the points around Buck Ridge. So, we rode to Buck Ridge Cabin from the Windmill. 'Course, we packed all the way. We had some big horses and mules.

BUCK RIDGE CABIN

When we finally got into Buck Ridge Cabin that night, the snow was so deep that we were pushing snow up to the horses' throats. It was too late in the evening to do anything when we got there, so we just unpacked and turned the horses loose. We didn't even bother puttin' 'em in the corral--they weren't goin' anywhere. We figured they could get up against the cabin for a wind break. We tossed some hay and grain to the horses and spent the night in the cabin.

The next day, we tried going off down the trail to Taylor Cabin. But hell, we couldn't make it. We tried riding the mules down there, but even they'd fall down. So, we went back to Buck Ridge and stayed another night. The next morning, we went down Mooney Trail and around through Sycamore Basin, then way back up to Taylor Cabin. Hell, there was two or three feet of snow even at Taylor Cabin, but the cattle were doing okay. We rode around a day or two checking on 'em. Then we just left 'em there and headed for home. Well, that was the first winter Dolly and I were married, and I had to leave her alone, stuck at the ranch with four feet of snow. While I was gone, she ran out of butane and didn't have any heat. We didn't have a fireplace in the house at that time. She couldn't even heat water. She tried to drive our old Chevy truck out on the freeze one morning. But the ground didn't freeze enough, and she kept gettin' stuck. The snow was clear up over the front of the truck and it kept slidin' off the road. It took her three hours to get to the Windmill Ranch, just three miles away.

Once we met back up at the Windmill, we camped out there for a while. Hell, we couldn'tget back to our ranch by vehicle for more than a month! We had a bunch of calves at the house that had to be fed. So, one day, I rode horseback to the house and droves the calves back to the Windmill where we fed them with the Miller's calves.

*****

It was around that time that I quit the DK and Dolly and I decided to give the Kingman ranch a try. On my mountain country ranch there, I had a good spring that ran off the south side of them mountain, mountains they call the Music Mountains. I had a lot of good dirt tanks down there, too. My neighbor to the north had a big spring on his land, but it was down under a hill. He had more land to the north of me, and in order to get the water to his land, he had to pump it across my land. So, we went into a partnership and bought a big pump and put it in a pipeline.

The government furnished the pipe for the state land, and we bought the pipe for the deeded land. The land was checkerboard. We owned a section and the government owned a section. That's 'cause of the railroad. When we first moved there, we owed the railroad twelve thousand dollars. We paid that off right away.

I worked that outfit all by myself. That's where I started using my cross-open...a brand. Sometimes, my neighbors helped me, and sometimes, I'd help them. I had good neighbors, both to the north and to the west. The Hualapai Indians were to the east. I never did work with the Indians, and they never worked with me.

I remember the fall of 1951. I left the house early one morning, way before daylight. I was lookin' for some lost cows, and I rode way up to the north end of the ranch. There had been some bad lightning storms the last couple of nights and really scattered the cattle. It took me most of the morning to work my way to the top of the Music Mountains. At about ten or eleven o'clock that morning, I topped out on one of the highest peaks around. I got down off my mare to let her blow, and I rolled myself a cigarette. I could see the country for miles around. It was a clear, pretty morning. I was lookin' off to the Northwest, enjoyin' the scenery, when all of a sudden, the whole horizon lit up in a bright flash. It scared the shit out of me! Then I realized I was watching one of them atomic bombs explode out there in the Nevada desert. I could actually feel the heat from it as I watched the big mushroom cloud grow in the sky. I never heard anything ever about it after that morning. But, you know, after that, Dolly started being sick a lot. And now I got this prostate cancer.

The nearest town to the ranch was the old mining town of Hackberry. We did some shoppin' there. Just for little things 'cause they didn't have much there. But that's where we got our mail once a month. I guess it was about forty miles of rough dirt road into Hackberry. We'd go into Kingman once in a while.

In the fall time, we'd go into Las Vegas and really load upon stuff. There was a good wholesale store there and 'cause we had a big storeroom at the ranch, we'd buy a whole truckload of stuff by the case. At the time, we had a real nice, brand new 1952 Chevy, three-quarter-ton pickup. It's the same one sitting behind the house now. Anyway, that's what we used to go into town about once a month. Sometimes, someone would bring our mail out to us.

One time, I went out to try and find a dozen or so cows that had got off into the hills, and I hadn't seen them for several weeks. I knew it might take a few days to find 'em all, so I packed up a big black gelding I had. I was ridin' a good stout chestnut mare I had just acquired. She was kindof green-broke, and I figured she could use the experience. So, we headed out.

For two days, I had seen almost no fresh signs of cows. Then, on the third day, I started to see fresh tracks, and I caught up with an old cow. I had a mixed bunch at that time. She was kind of a brindle colored, big and bad tempered. She had a good set of horns on her and I believed she might use 'em. I shook my rope out and made a wild run for her. She got out into an open flat and I got my rope over her head. I had a heavy four-strand rope and wasn't worried about her breaking it. She opened up her mouth a bellowin' and slobberin' and made a couple runs at me, but my little mare would side-step out of the way. I drug the cow towards the trees, and I managed to get my rope wrapped around a big pin on snag. I had her pulled up to the tree so that most of the rope was on my side. Her eyes were rollin,' and she was startin' to choke real bad. I was trying to get a halter on her head when she swung around and jammed her horn right into my left arm. When she jerked around again, the horn tore out of my arm, tearin' a big gash about four or five inches long, clear to the bone.

By this time, I was bleedin' like a stuck hog, so I left her tied up and headed for camp. My camp was right by a spring with a good cement spring box on it. I was covered with blood and hurtin' like hell when I cleaned the wound with a little piece of soap I carried in my saddle bags. I didn't have any kind of human medicine at all, but I did have a baking powder can be full of lime for doctorin' horses and cows. I pulled out my can of bacon grease from the cookin' gear and slathered that all over the wound before I sprinkled it with lime. The bleedin' had stopped, and the lime would keep the flies out of it, but, boy, did it burn!

I made myself some supper and rolled out my bedroll and tried to sleep. But it was hurtin' so bad I couldn't sleep. When I rolled out of bed in the mornin', my arm was swelled up so big I couldn't get it through the shirt sleeve. I laid my arm in icy spring water to try and get the throbbin' to stop, but it didn't help much. I figured I better try to get home, so I saddled and packed my horse. First, I had to go untie that damn cow 'cause I figured I might not be back for a while. The pain was throbbing clear up into my neck and head. On the way up the canyon, I could hear that old cow moanin' from miles away. I wanted to just shoot her when I got to her, but I cut her loose and then headed for home.

I believe that felt like the longest ride of my life. It probably took about six hours, but it felt like six days to me. I know I fainted a couple of times, but I never did fall out of the saddle. The packhorse I turned loose 'cause I knew she would just go home. I trusted my little mare to take me home, too. It was a little past dark when we finally pulled into the ranch.

Dolly helped me put the horses away. The pack horse had gone home before me, and 'course that scared the hell out of Dolly. Well, Dolly got me in the truck and drove me to the hospital in Kingman. They sewed me up and kept me there all night and let me go the next day. They said it had gotten infected and might have killed me had I waited much longer.

We had some hard times there at the Kingman ranch. But none of it was too hard, 'cause we always made it somehow. We even bought a few cows now and then even though we didn't have a lot of money.

The worst year was 1953 when it was so dry–we had some problems. The grass had driedup, and there was no feed or much water. There were some big fires out there and what grassthere was burned up. We lost a lot of baby calves and a few cows. We had just gotten a hundred head of new cattle then, and they were poor and sorry to start with. Damn, we must have lost a quarter of the calves that spring. It was a bad drought. When the momma cows would die, we'd end up with dogie calves. Sometimes, we'd have ten or twelve dogie calves at one time. Down at the water holes, there would be dead calves all over the place. There was a fence between us and the Indian Reservation, and sometimes, it would rain right up to that fence and stop.

We had all those dogie calves down at the barn, and Dolly would feed 'em. She was hand feedin' 'em with a baby bottle. When one of 'em would die, she'd cry and cry. It was really hard on her. The few water tanks had a little water, but there was no feed around 'em. The price of cattle at that time was so low that it didn't pay to haul feed to 'em. Besides, the roads were so bad, and we were so far out, I just couldn't haul feed. That was a bad year. We just about lost every damn thing that year–1953. It wasn't 'till later on I put that pipeline in with my neighbor that I moved all my cattle up there. Then, everything was mostly okay.

Dolly got real sick in the spring of 1954, and had to have all those operations. She had togo to Phoenix for those X-ray treatments. When she came home, she was in pretty bad shape.

Well, we owned the Kingman outfit, but still owned Red Canyon Ranch in Sedona, too. I decidedwe ought to sell one of 'em and get out of debt.

So, I asked Dolly, "Which one do you want to sell?"

"I want to sell this one and go back home to Red Canyon."

She didn't think she was going to make it. I think we were both pretty scared she was going to die. So, to please her, we sold the Kingman outfit.

We advertised the place and sold it in no time. The third guy who looked at it bought it.

    We sold out cattle and all and even made a little money.

RED CANYON RANCH 1990

RED CANYON RANCH

In the spring of 1955, we loaded up everything in the truck and Dolly's car. She had a big Cadillac that would hold a lot of stuff, and I had my horse trailer to haul my horses. Red Canyon Ranch had been sitting empty for about four years. We had started drilling a well before we left. Old Emery Vickers was supposed to be drilling that well. He was living in that little rock bunkhouse. He never did get the well finished and he had four years to do it. He'd work for a few days, then he'd go to town and get drunk 'till he ran out of money. Then he'd come back and drill a little more. The only water we had was that old rock tank under the rocks and that cistern well behind the house. Whenever that had water in it, we pumped it to the storage tank on the side of the hill. That's all we had for water in those days.

For a year or two, I just worked around the house. It took a lot of time and money, but I had to finish the well. I built that old wooden derrick for the drilling rig and hired a couple of guys to finish the drillin' for me. It ended up goin' thirteen hundred feet before we got good water there. I put in the pipe and storage tank. I also dug a ditch from the well to the house and put in a pipeline. We started out by trying to use the windmill, but it just wouldn't pull the water that far. So, I had to buy the old pump jack that's there now. I paid five hundred dollars for it. I worked on the house and built a new barn and rebuilt my corrals. I didn't go to work for anybody right away. We still had our small grazing permit, and we bought enough cows to fill it. The permit was around Red Canyon and up on the mountain at Barney Pasture. Once I got Red Canyon Ranch goin,' I went back to work for the DK. That was 1957.

We did all of our grocery shoppin' in Cottonwood. We never went to Sedona, there wasn't much there we needed. We'd go once a week, sometimes every two weeks. The roads were really bad in the wintertime, but we went in just the same. We had a little old gasoline cat (bulldozer) that we'd use sometimes. We sure didn't get much company, though.

    Dolly started to get sicker all the time, and we decided we needed to be closer to town and hospitals. In 1978, we put the ranch up for sale. We were both gettin' tired of drivin' that old road. I had to drive to the DK headquarters three or four times a week and didn't like leaving Dolly at home by herself. During that time, lots of Forest Service guys and those archaeologists from NAU started comin' out and takin' photographs. They'd give lectures and stuff like that. But they never really gave us any trouble. So, we sold out to the Fores Service andbought this place here in Sedona...

BARN AT RED CANYON RANCH

IN DUE TIME

In February of 1989, Joe died a lingering death from cancer in the hospital in Cottonwood, possibly from radiation exposure, when he witnessed the "Dog Detonation" near Kingman. Childless, he left his house and most everything to my dad. However, just before he died, a young cowgirl from the Windmill Ranch persuaded Joe to change his will and leave everything to her. She had convinced him that my dad's intentions were not genuine. We went to visit Joe in the hospital one time and found her straddled the old man cowgirl-style while he lay dying.

One rainy night a week after Joe died, my dad and I were on our way home to Red Canyon and passed by Joe's old house on Dry Creek Road. My dad pulled over and told me to wait in the truck. He climbed over the barbed wire fence and disappeared into the barn. He came trotting out with Joe's old saddle and bridle.

A couple of years before Joe died, my dad had been working for the Coconino National Forest as an archaeologist. He applied for the caretaker job at Red Canyon Ranch, which had been renamed Palatki Heritage Site for the well-preserved Sinaguan ruins there. It really wasn't a job; there was no salary.

Our rent was for the maintenance of the house and monitoring of the ruins. My dad was a shoe-in for the job and we moved there in 1987 with a gelding named Johnny that Joe had given us. We lived in Red Canyon until 1993. Although Red Canyon was originally homesteaded by the dry farmer, Charlie Willard, Joe's handiwork and brand were everywhere.

My dad was never able to keep his promise to Joe to go with him into Sycamore Canyon before he died, nor was he able to prevent his eventual death from cancer. But my dad had given him good company and friendship on those long days together on horseback. Other than the spring and fall roundups, most of the work Joe did for the DK and Windmill Ranches would have been solo if it weren't for my dad being along. Joe Robinson was a window into a time that is both changed and gone. Being an old-time cowboy in Arizona was a very satisfying life for many. Joe belonged to that type, a generation of young men, mostly from Texas, who went looking for adventure further west. By the early 1900's, the open range and long cattle drives in Texas were coming to an end. The range had been fenced up. Arizona and New Mexico were the obvious choices for men who wanted to live and work in open country. Joe was a representative of this type who lived across Arizona from the mid-1800's to the late 1930's. He followed the chuck wagons on large cattle drives in Texas and Arizona. Open range, chuck wagons and large cattle drives are the three things that distinguish the old-time cowboy from the modern.

Today's cowboys will trailer a horse (if they use a horse instead of a four-wheeler) to the grazing allotment. After a day of opening and closing gates, they drive to their home full of modern conveniences. However, there are still cowboys who work from horseback and tend cattle on public lands. Aspects of cowboy culture survive and are kept alive by these few. Some generational ranching families have managed to hang on to grazing permits for over a hundred years. These families raise all-natural, steroid, and antibiotic-free beef. Ranching and it's accompanying culture survive in small pockets throughout the West. The greatest surviving influence today is the Western style of dress. From the high-heeled boots to the big hats, every part of the cowboy's dress served a function and had a practical purpose. Not only was it utilitarian, it distinguished them from other professions. However, now cities throughout the West have their share of people dressed in cowboy garb, most of whom have never sat atop a horse. This sentiment is best expressed by an old anecdote told by one of Joe's contemporaries:

A little tourist boy is visiting out West with his family and sees a man in a big hat and pointy-toed boots. He asks his mom, "Is that a real cowboy?" Mom answers, "I guess so, adding to herself, "or maybe he's just a bartender!"

One becomes hard pressed to think of any modern profession that would offer such freedoms as living outdoors and working from Horseback. It's this fulfilling lifestyle that has been mythologized and has captivated the American mind. It's no surprise that when my dad asked Joe if he had any regrets being a life-long cowboy, the answer was an emphatic, "Hell no! Not once, ever!"

Printed in the USA
CPSIA information can be obtained
at www.ICGtesting.com
CBHW052019281124
17860CB00098B/194

9 798330 517213